God's ????
Foreknowledge
& Man's
Free Will

God's ????
Foreknowledge
& Man's
Free Will

RICHARD RICE

BETHANY HOUSE PUBLISHERS
MINNEAPOLIS, MINNESOTA 55438
A Division of Bethany Fellowship, Inc.

About the Author

Richard Rice received his Ph.D. in Systematic Theology from the University of Chicago Divinity School. He is an ordained minister with pastoral experience. He presently teaches university courses in Theology and Philosophy of Religion.

Originally titled *The Openness of God*.

Published by Bethany House Publishers
A Division of Bethany Fellowship, Inc.
6820 Auto Club Road, Minneapolis, Minnesota 55438

Printed in the United States of America

Library of Congress Cataloging in Publication Data

Rice, Richard, 1944-
    God's foreknowledge and man's free will.

    Rev. ed. of: The openness of God. © 1980.
    Includes bibliographical references.
    1. God—Omniscience. 2. Predestination.
3. Free will and determinism. 4. Freedom (Theology)
I. Rice, Richard, 1944-   . Openness of God. II. Title.
BT131.R53   1985   231   85-13330
ISBN 0-87123-845-4

Dedication

To Gail, who shares God's love for life.

Preface

Richard Rice's book represents a virtuoso piece of thinking. There's hardly a page on which I haven't underlined several sentences, often with paragraphs circled and stars in the margin. The introduction alone is classic—for his articulate warning against the dangers of using piety as a cover for intellectual laziness.

He has put his finger on a painfully sensitive spot in our theology and has probed it responsibly. I can't say I agree with Rice completely—but then I doubt that ready agreement is even desirable for a thesis as provocative as this. More useful is an open mind and a willingness to give it a workout. Even if you disagree with his conclusions, you have to admit that they're honestly taken.

John Boykin
Author of *Circumstances and the Role of God*
published by Zondervan

Contents

Introduction

"Does God know everything that's going to happen to me? Can He foresee all my actions and decisions? Did He know Adam would sin when He created him? Does He know now who will be saved and who will be lost?"

Every pastor and religious educator has heard these questions. And even those only mildly interested in religion have asked them at one time or another. They reflect what may be the most fundamental issues in religion, namely, the question of God's relation to the world and the question of human freedom. And they may be the most difficult of all questions to resolve, since any answer seems to leave us in a quandary. If, on the one hand, God knows all our actions in advance, how can we be free? On the other hand, if He doesn't, how can He be perfect? How could there be anything He doesn't know?

This book is concerned with how God experiences the world. It also discusses the closely related questions of human freedom and divine foreknowledge. It is, therefore, an essay in systematic theology. Some people feel that although everyone should respond to God, trained theologians should do the thinking about Him. But they are mistaken. Thinking about God is everyone's responsibility (Matt. 22:37; 1 Pet. 3:15). Theological reflection is much too important to leave to the professionals. Moreover, it is inevitable. We all have ideas about what is ultimately important in life, and we all have basic apprehensions about the nature of reality. At bottom, these are theological questions. In fact, the great questions of life are all theological questions. Every one of them is affected by our belief as to whether or not there is a God, and if so, what kind of being He is. So we are all theologians at one time or another, whether we realize it or not.

Our understanding of God has enormous practical significance as well. What we think of God and how we respond to Him are closely related. An inaccurate view of God can have disastrous effects on personal religious experience. We could never love a hostile, tyrannical being, though He might terrify us into submission. And we could not respect a mild, indulgent figure who never took us seriously. Our personal religious experience can be healthy only if we hold an adequate conception of God.

At the same time, our own experience will have an indelible effect on what we think of God. Some things we could never believe, because they radically contradict our experience of God. Hence, the bumper sticker, "God is not dead—I talked to Him this morning." The affirmation doesn't prove that God exists. But it shows that some people find it impossible to doubt His existence. Others have suffered a disastrous experience that makes it difficult for them to confess the beneficence, or even the reality, of God.

This discussion suggests an alternative to the traditional Christian understanding of God's relation to the world. Its central thesis is that reality itself and consequently God's experience of reality are essentially open rather than closed. This means that God experiences the events of the world He has created—especially the events of human history—as they happen, rather than all at once in some timeless, eternal perception. This also means that not even God knows the future in all its details. Some parts remain indefinite until they actually occur, and so they can't be known in advance. Otherwise, as we shall see, the idea of freedom is meaningless. Although this thesis varies from the conventional Christian view of God's relation to the world, it has the support of both the Bible and religious experience. It makes more sense on a rational basis as well. In addition, the open view of God ultimately enriches such concepts as divine providence, prophecy, and foreknowledge.

Such an understanding of God's relation to the world does not really represent a departure from the essential Christian concept of God. Indeed, it is more faithful to the biblical portrait of God than the more widely accepted view, as the following discussion will show. Its starting point is the transcendent-personal God of the Christian tradition. So it assumes, without attempting to establish, the general validity of the customary Christian concept. And it revises this concept only to render it more internally consistent and to bring it into clearer harmony with the Bible. Our objective is to formulate a concept of God that remains as close to the Christian tradition as possible. Therefore, our fundamental perspective is that of conservative Christianity. The discussion takes for granted conventional concepts like predictive prophecy and divine intervention in the creaturely world.

Since the topic concerns people of every background, this discussion does not presuppose theological training on the reader's part. The book is intended for that elusive figure, the interested layman, who though by no means a theological specialist, nevertheless thinks deeply at times and willingly follows an argument to its conclusion. I have done my best to avoid technicalities as much as possible. At the same time, I have tried not to oversimplify the issues raised. Oversimplification is usually worse than confusion. To ease the flow of thought, I have also kept footnotes to a minimum.

Our discussion begins with a consideration of the conventional understanding of God's relation to the world and the difficulties that it involves. The two subsequent chapters explain the open view of God and its biblical support. Chapters that follow relate the open view of God to the concepts of divine foreknowledge, providence, prophecy, and predestination. In the last chapter we shall assess the value of the open view of God for personal religious experience.

A final word on the appropriateness of this undertaking: Any study of God needs to avoid two pitfalls. First, we must recognize the danger of presumption. We tend to exaggerate our ability to understand God. Often we insist that He conform to our ideas about Him. The less appreciated danger is to exaggerate our inability to understand God. Some people insist that we know hardly anything about God because He is "beyond" all human thought. The first danger leads ultimately to anthropomorphism—the view that God is just a glorified human being. The second leads ultimately to agnosticism—the view that we know nothing about God at all.

In general, Christians today are more guilty of the second than of the first of these errors. Some even use piety as a cover for intellectual laziness. Any student of the nature of God soon recognizes the inadequacy of human thought to this great subject. But to say that we can never understand the nature of God is appropriate only after we have strained our powers to the fullest. It is acceptable as a conclusion to rigorous intellectual work but not as an excuse for neglecting it.

Deuteronomy 29:29 suggests the proper attitude, and it lies between these undesirable extremes. "The secret things belong to the Lord our God; but the things that are revealed belong to us and to our children for ever." Revelation defines the appropriate scope of theological reflection. Our attempt to understand God should begin and end with what God has disclosed about Himself. Accordingly, to inquire beyond what God has revealed is presumptuous, but to rest satisfied with less than all that God has revealed is irresponsible.

1

The Conventional
View of God

In this chapter we shall examine the customary understanding of God's relation to the world. Generalizations are never exact, and this one is no exception. No precise concept of God's relation to the world has received unanimous Christian assent. Theologians wrestle with the question in their own distinctive ways, and believers in general may never formulate it in precise conceptual terms. On the other hand, Christians typically prefer certain ways to others regarding God's relation to the world. And it always helps in attempting to revise something to describe what needs revision.

Accordingly, the view of God's relation to the world (variously identified in this discussion as "traditional," "conventional," "customary," "classical," and so on) resembles the "ideal types" employed in works like H. Richard Niebuhr's *Christ and Culture*. As Niebuhr points out, a "type" is an artificial construct. It is never perfectly exemplified in any actual person or group. It only approximates the thinking or behavior of people. Nevertheless, a type is a useful interpretive device since the resemblances and differences among various viewpoints do fall into a general pattern.[1] The view of God discussed here is not intended

---

[1]H. Richard Niebuhr, *Christ and Culture* (New York: Harper & Row, Publishers, 1951), pp. 43, 44.

to represent precisely the position of any specific theologian or Christian community. It refers instead to a way of looking at God that most Christians take for granted. It is the view prevalent in the mainstream of historic Christian theology.

The customary view of God has two essential features. One is the belief that God is completely aware of the creaturely world and is intimately involved in the course of creaturely events. The other is the conviction that God is utterly changeless in all aspects of His being, including His knowledge of the world. In the following paragraphs we shall explore the logic of this understanding of God. In so doing we shall discover some of its basic difficulties.

The Bible describes God as perfect (Matt. 5:48). And the traditional understanding of God's relation to the world is closely related to a particular concept of perfection. In this view, a perfect being enjoys every positive quality to the maximum degree. Hence, God's holiness, faithfulness, and love could not possibly increase. And His wisdom and power are likewise incapable of improvement. In short, a perfect being simply cannot change. In the language of classical theology, God is "immutable."

 The logic of this view goes like this. Something can change in one of two ways—for the better or for the worse. Now God is in every conceivable respect the best it is possible to be, so He could hardly change for the better. If He changed at all, it could only be for the worse. The susceptibility to any kind of change, therefore, is incompatible with the idea of perfection. A perfect being must be absolutely changeless. In every respect, then, God is incapable of being anything other than exactly what He is. Otherwise, He would be less than perfect.

The notion of divine immutability draws apparent support both from certain biblical statements and from the requirements of personal religious experience.

Several texts speak of divine changelessness. "I the Lord do not change" (Mal. 3:6). "Jesus Christ is the same yesterday and today and for ever" (Heb. 13:8). "Every good endowment and every perfect gift is from above, coming down from the Father of lights with whom there is no variation or shadow due to change" (James 1:17).

Personal religious experience also seems to support the idea that God does not change. God is a constant source of strength to the faithful (Ps. 46:1; 91). He never fails those who trust in Him (Deut. 31:6, 8; Josh. 1:5; Isa. 43:1–2; 49:15–16; Heb. 13:5). And if God is absolutely reliable, then He must be unchangeable. For if He could change, how could we trust Him? How could we place in Him the unreserved commitment that He commands? Only a God who cannot change, it seems, will satisfy the requirements of personal religious experience.

The concept that divine perfection entails changelessness has important consequences for God's relation to the temporal world. If absolutely nothing in God changes, then the content of God's knowledge and experience must remain eternally the same—like everything else in God. Accordingly, God takes in all temporal reality—past, present, and future—in a single glance. He sees all in one timeless perception. Past and future in all their detail are equally open to His gaze. Indeed, He knows no "past" or "future." In one eternal present He comprehends all reality.

One of Augustine's interpreters describes the influential theologian's concept of God's relation to the world. The description clearly illustrates the familiar Christian view:

> In one single unchangeable glance God contemplates every being, every truth, every possible or real object. This knowledge is an eternal intuition before which the past and the future are as real as the present, but each for that portion of time in which it really exists. God encompasses all time and therefore can know the future as infallibly as He knows the present.[2]

John Calvin held essentially the same view of God's relation to the temporal world. Notice his definition of foreknowledge:

> When we attribute foreknowledge to God, we mean that all things always were, and perpetually remain, under his eyes, so that to his knowledge there is nothing future or past, but all things are present. And they are present in such a way that he not only conceives them through ideas, as we have before us those things which our minds remember, but he truly looks upon them and discerns them as things placed before him. And

---

[2]Eugene Portalie, *A Guide to the Thought of St. Augustine,* translated by Ralph J. Bastian (Chicago: Henry Regnery Company, 1960), p. 128.

this foreknowledge is extended throughout the universe to every creature.[3]

As Calvin's statement clearly shows, the customary view of God's relation to the world entails the concept of absolute foreknowledge. It implies that God knows the future in all its detail. Indeed, the classic view of foreknowledge is simply the description of God's knowledge of the future that logically follows from the concept of static perfection. For if a changeless God has infallible knowledge of reality, then His knowledge must also be changeless. It cannot increase or decrease. Accordingly, God never "learns" anything. He simply knows it. Nothing ever "enters God's experience." God's experience always already contains it.

Proponents of absolute foreknowledge account for it in one of two ways. According to some, God has absolute foreknowledge because He exercises absolute control. In Calvin's view, for example, God not only knows everything that will ever happen, but also everything happens the way it does because He wills it to be so. Calvin's famous doctrine of double predestination reflects this position:

> We call predestination God's eternal decree, by which he compacted with himself what he willed to become of each man. For all are not created in equal condition; rather, eternal life is foreordained for some, eternal damnation for others. Therefore, as any man has been created to one or the other of these ends, we speak of him as predestined to life or to death.[4]

According to Calvin, then, God plans everything that happens. His control over reality is absolute and all-inclusive. Nothing occurs that He has not ordained. This position assigns the origin of sin and suffering to God, and this seems incompatible with divine goodness and love. Calvin agrees that the reasons for sin and suffering are inscrutable to man. But, he insists, because God is in absolute control and because sin and suffering are real, they must have an integral part in God's plan.

Other Christians believe in absolute foreknowledge without

---

[3]John Calvin, *Institutes of the Christian Religion,* III. XXI. 5, translated by Ford Lewis Battles (Philadelphia: The Westminster Press, 1960), 2:926.
[4]*Ibid.*

subscribing to predestination. In their view <u>God knows the future infallibly,</u> not because He controls it absolutely but simply because He sees ahead of time what is going to happen. And everyday experience confirms that knowing what's going to happen does not make one responsible for what happens.

One afternoon a few years ago, for example, I watched my two-year-old son begin to run down a sloping sidewalk several yards away. I knew immediately that he would fall before he could stop himself. Yet I could not prevent the minor accident that soon occurred. My "foreknowledge" of his fall did not make me responsible for it. The causes of the occurrence were quite independent of my knowledge. Just so, the argument goes, <u>God's knowledge of the future does not make Him responsible for what happens.</u> As God says of the angelic rebels in John Milton's *Paradise Lost,* <u>"If I foreknew, Foreknowledge had no influence on their fault, Which had no less proved certain unforeknown."[5]</u>

Obviously, on the first view of divine foreknowledge the course of future events is already definite. Everything happens in accordance with an invariable divine plan. God is really the only agent. Everyone else plays the role God assigns. But it is not so obvious that the future is just as definite in the second view of divine foreknowledge. According to this view, God does not determine the course of events. He simply witnesses it in advance. Nonetheless, the net effect on the future is the same. It is closed, settled, invariable, in every detail. The real question, then, is not whether God has decided everything that will happen. The real question is whether the future is definite or not. Is everything that will happen already settled?

The following reasons indicate why the future is definite and why reality is closed in any view of absolute foreknowledge. By definition, perfect knowledge must reflect its object perfectly. It must correspond precisely to what it knows. So, if God's knowledge of the world is perfect, it must correspond precisely to the course of creaturely events. If, however, God's knowledge is also changeless, then the object of His knowledge must itself be

---

[5]John Milton, *Paradise Lost,* Book III, lines 117–119; *The Portable Milton* (New York: The Viking Press, 1949), p. 292.

changeless, too, since God's knowledge perfectly reflects it. The view that God's knowledge of the world is changeless thus requires the conclusion that reality too is changeless. It is fixed or closed. Nothing could be other than it is.

Consequently, if we attribute to God knowledge of the future that is both changeless and exhaustive, we must conceive the entire course of events as changeless too. For if God knows the future exhaustively, then the future in all its detail is there to be known. It must be as definite as God's knowledge of it. If the future is absolutely foreknowable, then, it is just as definite and just as settled as if God had planned it down to the last detail. Everything that will happen shall happen. Whether or not we hold God directly responsible for it all is quite beside the central point.

Jonathan Edwards forcefully expresses this point in somewhat different terms. In his treatise *Freedom of the Will*, Edwards refutes Arminian notions of freedom on the grounds that they are excluded by God's absolute foreknowledge. In his words, "all certain knowledge proves the necessity of the truth known; whether it be before, after, or at the same time." "Whether prescience be the thing that *makes* the event necessary or no, it alters not the case. Infallible foreknowledge may *prove* the necessity of the event foreknown, and yet not be the thing which *causes* the necessity."[6]

This line of reasoning also reveals that the concept of absolute foreknowledge results in the ultimate collapse of all temporal distinctions. If God's knowledge of the future is as definite as His knowledge of the past, and if His knowledge is the perfect reflection of reality, then the future itself is just as definite as the past. There is therefore no ultimate difference between the past and the future.

The apparent difference between past and future thus does not reflect the nature of reality. Instead, it springs from the limitations of our creaturely perspective. The reason human beings do not know the future is not that it is not there to be known,

---

[6]Jonathan Edwards, *Freedom of the Will*, ed. Paul Ramsey (New Haven and London: Yale University Press, 1957), pp. 266, 263 (italics original).

but that we are not in a position to witness it.[7] Temporal distinctions pertain to our acquisition of knowledge but not to the content of reality. "Past" and "future" thus simply designate different portions of reality as they appear to us. That part of reality which we designate "the past" is relatively accessible to human knowledge, whereas the contrasting portion, "the future," remains relatively inaccessible. We find the future unknowable because we lack the faculties to perceive it, not because it isn't there yet.

The view of reality that absolute foreknowledge requires is sometimes described as the "spatializing" of time. It conceives of time as if it were space, simultaneously extended in all its dimensions. Imagine yourself standing on a brick wall eight feet high. A friend works in the garden below you and behind the wall. From your vantage point you can see things that the wall obscures from his view. You can see the traffic in the street and the landscape beyond. Similarly, our limited, finite perspective keeps the future unknowable. It lies beyond the range of our perceptual field. In contrast, God enjoys a sufficiently exalted vantage point to be free of these limitations. So He can see the future. What is obscured from our view is clear to Him. The future only appears indefinite or undecided to us because we cannot see it as it is. But this indefiniteness or undecidedness is illusory. It arises from the limitations of our finite perspective.

When we see that the idea of absolute foreknowledge (1) follows from a static concept of perfection and (2) results in a closed view of reality, the chief difficulty of the traditional understanding of God's relation to the temporal world comes clearly into view. This is the fact that it excludes creaturely freedom.

As Chapter 3 describes more fully, the Bible affirms the reality of creaturely freedom in a great many ways. The most obvious are passages directly calling for personal decision. These include the strong appeals of Moses (Deut. 30:19), Joshua (Josh. 24:15), and Elijah (1 Kings 18:21) to the people of Israel to serve the Lord. The numerous commands (Gen. 2:16, 17; Ex. 20:3–17),

---

[7]To use technical terms, temporal distinctions have epistemological or psychological, but not ontological, reference.

invitations (Isa. 55:6, 7; Matt. 11:28), and warnings (Ezek. 33:11) recorded in Scripture also imply the reality of human freedom, as do straightforward descriptions of personal responsibility (Eccl. 12:13, 14; Ezek. 18:1–4).

We can describe freedom in several ways. At the very least, freedom involves the absence of external compulsion. A person compelled to act by something or someone else has not acted freely. However, some people limit their definition of *freedom* to free acts that flow spontaneously from the nature of a being. According to this view, the *essential* quality of freedom is the absence of external coercion. So as long as an act flows naturally from the constitution of a being, it is free.

This concept of freedom harmonizes with the idea of absolute divine foreknowledge. For if freedom is merely the absence of external compulsion, a creature's future actions may be entirely predicted by anyone sufficiently acquainted with that creature. Possessing exhaustive knowledge of every person's inner workings, God would thus know everything everyone would ever do.

According to this way of thinking, the complete predictability of one's actions does not negate personal freedom as long as the actions flow from internal and not external causes. Absolute foreknowledge thus arises from God's exhaustive knowledge of the present. For if the course of future events follows entirely from factors that are already present, then anyone who exhaustively knows the present can predict the future with infallible accuracy. Since God does know the present exhaustively, He knows infallibly all that will ever happen.

This explanation of absolute foreknowledge is unacceptable, however, because the definition of freedom involved is inadequate. Freedom requires more than the absence of coercion. It also requires the presence of genuine alternatives, as personal experience indicates. To take a trivial example, when I enter my closet to select a shirt to wear, my intuition is that my decision is something made at that moment. My choice is not the outworking of unknown internal causes. I *make* the choice. I don't simply find out what I was destined to do by factors of which I am unaware. A free act or decision renders definite something that was previously indefinite. In a genuinely free decision something really *becomes*. It is not merely discovered. If "what shirt I shall wear on Tuesday" is something I really decide at 7:30 on the morning in question, then it must remain indefinite until that moment in history. If not, then I don't really decide it. Instead, I simply find it out at the time. Only if something becomes definite as a consequence of my choice does it represent a free decision.

Someone might argue that conscious experience is essentially the same whether I actually make a decision or only think that I do. But that does not substantially change our line of reasoning. The question is not whether I think I am free but whether I am in fact free. To be sure, I may think that I am making a decision when in reality my selection is already determined by factors of which I am not aware. It is conceivable that my choice of shirts, for example, is already determined. And this may be the case with many of our supposedly free decisions. But if this is true of *all* our choices, then we really have no freedom at all. Our decisions contribute nothing to reality. We are merely under the illusion that they do because our knowledge is limited.

The fact that freedom entails indefiniteness makes it fundamentally incompatible with absolute foreknowledge, for the classic view of divine foreknowledge requires a definite or closed view of reality. If God knows the future in all its detail—either because it is already there, or because everything that will happen is the inevitable outcome of factors already present—then supposedly free decisions contribute nothing to reality. They simply underline the limited knowledge of finite beings. If God's knowledge of the future is exhaustive, then the entire future is definite, and creaturely freedom is an illusion.

A frequent response to this objection to absolute foreknowledge is the observation that you can predict someone's decisions with a high degree of accuracy if you are well acquainted with his habits and preferences. An attentive man may know that his wife will choose cotton over polyester. He may know that his son will elect to play baseball rather than soccer. But in neither case does his advance knowledge render the decision empty. His wife and son still remain free to choose. It is just that what they will choose is foreknowable to one who knows their habits and personalities well enough. So, it is argued, foreknowledge does not exclude genuine freedom.

Such a response misses the point. *An act is free precisely to the extent that it renders definite something otherwise indefinite.* If indeed a person's choice of, say, pumpkin pie rather than chocolate cake is predictable with absolute certainty, then it is questionable whether that particular decision is really free. The person may be reacting to ingrained impulses or to well-established habits, in which case his response to a given set of alternatives is already decided. Instead of making a free decision at the time, he is merely experiencing the effects of decisions he made long before.

Except for die-hard Calvinists, most Christians affirm a world characterized by the presence of genuine freedom. At the same time, however, most Christians also accept the view that God is utterly immutable and has exhaustive knowledge of the future. We have just seen that we cannot have it both ways. The customary conception of God's relation to the temporal world logically exludes the possibility of freedom. Calvinism has the merit of logical consistency, at least on this point. If we want to affirm freedom, therefore, we shall have to consider another conception of God.

There is another objection to the idea of static perfection and to the concept of absolute foreknowledge. Static perfection is incompatible with the essential divine attribute of love (see John 3:16; 16:27; Rom. 5:8; 1 John 4:8). Love involves interest in and concern for the object of love. It also involves sensitivity to the experiences of the beloved. A loving father, for example, will be affected differently by the different experiences of his child. His level of concern will remain constant. But the content of his actual experience will vary with the child's situation. He will rejoice with the child who rejoices and weep with the child who weeps.

From beginning to end, the Bible portrays God as infinitely sensitive to the creaturely world. The Old Testament describes God's reaction to the moral decline of the antediluvians (Gen. 6:6) and the apostasy of the chosen people (Hos. 11:8) in highly emotional language. Jesus further emphasized God's responsiveness to His creations. According to His greatest parables,

God rejoices when sinners repent (Luke 15:7, 10). Indeed, God takes note when a sparrow falls and even numbers the very hairs of our heads (Matt. 10:29, 30).

Such momentary sensitivity of the one who loves to the experiences of the beloved is impossible for God if we hold the view of static perfection, for it attributes to God exhaustive knowledge of the future. And if all future events are already data in God's knowledge, then their actual occurrence contributes nothing new to His experience. He does not share the experiences of His creatures *as they occur.* Instead, He enjoys the entire value of creaturely reality at once.

Supporters of the conventional view may argue that absolute divine foreknowledge does not mean that the actual occurrence of an event makes no difference to God. The common view only insists that He knows ahead of time everything that will happen. Donald Bloesch, for example, claims that "although God knows the future before it happens, he does not literally know the concrete event until it happens."[8] But this attributes a distinction to the divine consciousness that absolute foreknowledge rules out. For if God has absolute knowledge of the future and if He knows all that will ever happen, then He surely knows in full detail the contents of His own experience. And if He knows exactly not only what will happen but also how He will respond to every situation, then, in effect, He already has the experience. The actual occurrence of events makes no new contribution to His experience. It is, therefore, impossible to attribute both absolute foreknowledge and momentary sensitivity to God. The two are fundamentally incompatible.

The static view of divine perfection and the concept of absolute foreknowledge that it entails are fraught with difficulties. By denying God's relationship to time they exclude the possibility of genuine creaturely freedom and evacuate the attribute of love of an essential component when applied to God. This concept of God has far more in common with the "unmoved mover" of Aristotle than with the God of the Bible. An exami-

---

[8]Donald G. Bloesch, *Essentials of Evangelical Theology,* Vol. One: "God, Authority, and Salvation" (New York: Harper & Row, Publishers, 1978), p. 29.

nation of its history would uncover roots in Greek rather than Hebrew soil. Its prevalence in Christian theology offers yet another testimony to the enormous impact of that stream of ancient thought on the doctrines of the church. Fortunately, it is not the only view of God available.

2

The Open View of God

In the preceding chapter we examined the conventional understanding of God's relation to the world and reviewed some of its problems. We saw that when perfection is conceived of as absolute changelessness, God's experience of the world must also be absolutely changeless. And this means that the world itself is essentially changeless too. It is closed rather than open. Nothing could be other than it is.

The most serious consequence of this view for Christian thought is that it excludes creaturely freedom. For if reality is closed, there are no genuine alternatives. And without genuine alternatives nothing is left for the creature to decide. We may think we are making decisions or selecting among different options at frequent points in our experience, but this is only because our perspective is limited. In reality everything that happens, including our "choices" or "decisions," is already definite.

An alternate way of thinking about God's relation to the world avoids the tremendous difficulties of the conventional view. Furthermore, it better represents the biblical idea of God. We shall call it the "open view of God." This chapter will outline its basic features and describe some of its advantages.

The central claim of this alternate view is that God's experience of the world is open rather than closed. God's experience does not consist of one timeless intuition. He does not have one eternal perception of all reality, past and future. Instead, He responds to developments and changes in the world as they occur. Accordingly, God is open to new experiences and receives new stimuli. He continuously assimilates new data. God does not have once and for all the entire value of the creaturely world. He acquires the value of creaturely events as they happen, as they come into existence.

Another way to make the point is to say that time is real for God. His experience is the *infallible* register of temporal reality. It reflects every event and development in the temporal world. All that happens enters His memory and is retained forever. Nothing escapes His notice. But God's experience is also the *progressive* register of reality. Events enter His experience as they happen, not before. This means that God experiences the past and the future differently. They are not the same for Him. He remembers the past exhaustively, in all its detail. Every aspect is vividly present to His mind. But His experience of the future is different. He anticipates the future, to be sure, and in a way unique to Him, as we shall see. But the future retains its essential indefiniteness from God's perspective as well as from ours.

The openness of God thus denotes God's reception of new experiences. It indicates His capacity for novelty. It refers to the progressive character of God's relation to the temporal world.

Behind the open view of God lies a twofold conception of the Divine Being. In light of His relation to the creaturely world, we have asserted that God's experience of temporal reality is progressive, developmental, and thus open. But this openness involves only one aspect of God, namely, His experience. There is another aspect of His being to which it does not apply, for there are certain ways in which He is utterly unaffected by the world and incapable of or insusceptible to any kind of development or change. In those respects that distinguish God from all other forms of reality, He could not conceivably be other than exactly what He is. One such respect is God's existence.

The first and most fundamental description of God in the Bible is of His creative activity: "In the beginning God created the heavens and the earth" (Gen. 1:1). The biblical doctrine of creation includes both an account of the origin of the world and a conception of God's continuing relation to creaturely reality.

Scripture describes God as preserving the heavens as well as making the earth and the seas, with all their inhabitants (Neh. 9:6). He is the momentary source of human life: "In him we live and move and have our being" (Acts 17:28).

To speak of God as Creator is to say that He is the source of reality. From Him alone everything derives its existence. While everything owes its existence to God, however, He, the ultimate source of life, does not owe His own existence to anyone or anything else. In other words, God is self-existent. He is the one being who would exist whether anything else existed or not.

In temporal terms, all other beings come into existence at some point in time. They are capable of ceasing to exist or subject to nonexistence. But it is impossible to think of God as either coming into existence or as ever ceasing to exist. We can think of God only as existing. (This was the point of Anselm's famous argument.) God was here before anything else existed. He would still be here if everything else vanished. In the words of the Psalm, "Before the mountains were brought forth, or ever thou hadst formed the earth and the world, from everlasting to everlasting thou art God" (90:2). Properly speaking, then, God alone is immortal (1 Tim. 6:16). God's existence is thus one aspect of the Divine Being that is unaffected by the creaturely world. When we say that God is open, therefore, we do not mean that He is open to nonexistence.

The divine character is also unaffected by the world. God's character refers to the kind of person God is. It involves His fundamental disposition or attitude toward the creaturely world. The Bible attributes to God such personal qualities as faithfulness (1 Cor. 1:9), righteousness (Ps. 11:7), justice (Zeph. 3:5), and mercy (Ex. 34:6, 7). When we deny that God's character is open, we mean that nothing about these attributes could conceivably be different. The fact that God possesses these qualities and the precise nature of these qualities are unaffected by the events in the creaturely world. What makes God God (that which distinguishes Him essentially from all other forms of reality) is thus absolutely unchangeable. Correctly, the classical view of God has always insisted on this.

We can illustrate this respect in which God is changeless by considering briefly the single attribute that best expresses the essential content of God's character. "God is love" (1 John 4:8). The English word *love* is notoriously inexact. It covers an enormous range of experiences. It can refer to the most profound commitment between human beings or to our preferences in food, clothing, and entertainment. However, the language the New Testament writers used, Koine Greek, included several words for love. They were, therefore, much more precise when they attributed love to God.

In his well-known discussion of the Christian concept of love, entitled *Agapē and Eros,* Swedish theologian Anders Nygren distinguishes between the conceptions of love expressed by these two Greek words. He argues that the New Testament applies only *agapē* to God. In the *eros* sense of love certain qualities or features in the object of love make it attractive to the lover, who desires to possess it. But in the case of *agapē* the lover is motivated not by attractive qualities in the beloved or by a desire to possess the object. *Agapē* is self-giving. Its only motive is the welfare of its object.[1]

In attributing *agapē* to God the New Testament writers emphasized God's unselfish concern for the welfare of His creatures. In their view, His love consists in His unchanging desire for their best interest. According to 1 John, God's love takes the initiative; it is aggressive: "In this is love, not that we loved God but that he loved us . . ." (4:10); "We love, because he first loved us" (4:19). In the words of Paul, "God shows his love for us in that while we were yet sinners Christ died for us" (Rom. 5:8). For the apostles, the unselfish character of God's love is best seen in the fact that He loves the totally undeserving.

When we say that God's love is changeless or unaffected by

---

[1]The Translator's Preface to the English edition nicely summarizes Nygren's distinction: "Eros is an appetite, a yearning desire, which is aroused by the attractive qualities of its object. . . . Agapē is . . . distinguished from Eros in that it is 'indifferent to value.' That is to say, it is neither kindled by the attractiveness nor quenched by the unattractiveness of its object. This is seen most clearly in God's love for sinners, who are loved in spite of their sin. . . . His loving is not determined by the worthiness or unworthiness of those whom He loves, but by His own nature of love" (*Agapē and Eros,* translated by Philip S. Watson [New York: Harper & Row, Publishers, 1969], pp. xvi–xvii).

the creaturely world, we mean that His interest or concern for His creatures never varies. It remains at one level of intensity. God never acts out of less than complete commitment to the welfare of His creatures. Their well-being is always foremost in His mind. To say that God's character is changeless means that the quality of His relationships is constant. He always relates to His creatures in the same way. It does not mean, of course, that the content of God's actual relations is always the same. In fact, it requires exactly the opposite, for the more one person loves another and the more constant is the level of his concern, the more varied will be the content of his actual experience.

Consider the difference between a good parent and a poor parent. A parent who loves a child perfectly will never fail to respond to the child's experiences. And because the level of his sensitivity to the child is constant, or changeless, his actual experience of the child's life will be constantly developing. Nothing that brings the child joy or sadness will escape his notice. He will be touched with the child's hurts and disappointments. He will feel exhilarated by his joys. Since the quality of his relationship to his child is constant, his actual experiences of the child will vary. In contrast, a poor parent will be partially or wholly unresponsive to his child's experiences. He may be excited by his child's academic accomplishments but insensitive to his social needs. Or he may be utterly indifferent to anything that happens to the child, good or bad. So there seems to be a direct relation between the level of one's concern for someone else, on the one hand, and the degree to which one is affected by that person, on the other. The greater the concern, the higher the sensitivity.

God's love is supreme. Accordingly, it transcends all earthly affection, not in its lack of response to creaturely experience but in the infinite subtlety of its response. Changelessness in the face of changing experiences, not to be influenced or affected by the different and varying experiences of another, is not love. It represents indifference. To attribute supreme love to God, therefore, we should think of Him as supremely responsive to the experiences of His creatures. If God really loves me more than anyone else does, then any change in my life will not affect Him less than it affects others, it will affect Him more. Consequently, to say that God is perfect in love implies two things. First, it implies that His sensitivity to the world never changes. Second, it implies that His actual experience of the world never remains the same, since it responds perfectly to everything we undergo.

In the light of this twofold understanding of God, it becomes evident that the open view of God represents a less drastic departure from the customary conception of God than first appears to be the case. The options are not limited to a view of God who is entirely closed and a view of God who is entirely open. Instead of proposing a God whose being is closed in all respects, we are suggesting one whose being is open in one important respect. God remains open in His experience of the world, but His existence and His character remain changeless. And there is nothing contradictory in attributing both to God as long as we apply them to different aspects of His being.

The open view of God thus departs from the common concept in its attempt to reflect more adequately the biblical portrayal of God as intimately involved in and sensitive to the ongoing course of creaturely events. But it shares the familiar conception of God as the ultimate reality, whose existence and essential character are utterly unaffected by the creaturely world.

Unlike other beings, God's openness involves only His concrete experience of the creaturely world. It does not apply to either His existence or to His character. In addition, the very nature of God's openness also distinguishes Him from nondivine forms of reality. For one thing, the scope of God's experience radically differs from that of any creature, because it is unrestricted. God's experience includes literally all there is to know (1 John 3:20). Moreover, it is unrivaled in intensity or adequacy. Only God knows exhaustively. Every aspect of reality is perfectly represented only in His experience. Our knowledge, in contrast, is always partial and vague (1 Cor. 13:12). It is never fully adequate to its objects.

Furthermore, God's experience is open in only one sense, which further distinguishes His experience from ours. Creaturely knowledge can diminish as well as grow. We not only learn, but we also forget. And what we do remember we never remember perfectly. In contrast, God's memory is perfect. What He experiences He fully retains in His consciousness forever. Not one detail is ever lost. God's memory is therefore the infallible register of the past. His memory is the one place where all that has ever happened is retained in the full vividness of its concrete actuality. In only one sense, then, is God's experience open. It can only increase, never decrease. The open view of God, therefore, in no sense compromises the qualitative distinction between divine and creaturely reality. It stands squarely in the tradition that emphasizes God's transcendence of the creaturely world.

The open view of God presupposes an open view of reality itself, in which the concepts of time, novelty, and freedom are essential. According to this view of reality, the temporal world is an ongoing process of events that come into existence. It is not a collection of things that simply are what they are. Time—the passage of the future into the past—is characteristic of the actual nature of reality. Time is not a mere projection of the way we happen to experience the world. Moreover, as the ongoing occurrence of events, reality is also characterized by the emergence of novelty. Not everything that will happen is already determined. A significant portion of the future remains to be decided. The part now open consists of the future free decisions made by the creatures as well as by God. So, in the open view of reality creaturely freedom plays an important role.

Some people try to base a dynamic concept of God's experience on the curious notion that God chooses to remain ignorant of certain future events. According to this view, He could know the future exhaustively if He wanted to. It is there to be known. But He deliberately blocks certain events from His mind. In this way He can experience them as they occur, rather than all at once. This concept may seem to be an improvement on the traditional view of God's relation to the world. But it is unacceptable for a number of reasons.

First, although it denies absolute divine foreknowledge, it accepts the idea that the future is absolutely foreknowable. Everything that will ever happen is definite in all its detail. And a completely definite future is incompatible with genuine creaturely freedom, as we have seen. So this idea of God's relation to the world offers no solution to one of the greatest difficulties of the conventional view. It, too, is incompatible with genuine creaturely freedom.

Second, the concept of selective divine ignorance denies that God enjoys perfect knowledge. He does not know everything there is to know. In contrast, theists have always maintained that one of the defining attributes of God is His having perfect knowledge. For God to be God He *must* know everthing He *could* know. He must know everything knowable. Consequently, a divine knowledge that is less than perfect is a contradiction in terms. (Chaper 5 will explain why the open view of God does not deny perfect knowledge to God.)

Third, it is hard to understand just what *selective ignorance* could possibly mean. Does it mean "forgetting," eliminating from consciousness something previously known? Was God's knowledge of the future exhaustive at one time and then less extensive as He deliberately forgot certain items? If so, how far can we carry this? Would God remember *that* He forgot? It is hard to see how He could, without also remembering *what* He forgot. And just how much would God have to forget to remain effectively ignorant of any one thing? At best the idea of deliberate forgetting is difficult to conceive. But it seems utterly impossible to apply to God.

Our critique of the conventional view of God's relation to the world shows the impossibility of affirming a static divine experience and a dynamic creaturely world. In effect, this concept does just the opposite. It holds that God's experience is dynamic while the creaturely world is static. But its results are no more satisfactory. It, too, presents us with confusion and contradiction.

In the final analysis, the concept of God's relation to the world proposed here is the only one that is logically coherent and faithful to our fundamental human experience. It views *both* the creaturely world *and* God's experience of it in dynamic rather than static terms.

Impressive philosophical evidence supports the open view of God and reality. But since our concern is theological rather than philosophical, we shall turn to the biblical evidence. We will begin with the earliest account of the creation of the world.

Process Theism and the Open View of God

Readers familiar with contemporary Christian theology will notice a resemblance between the view of God presented here and the concept of God found in the writings of Alfred North Whitehead, Charles Hartshorne, and their followers. Consequently, it will be helpful to spell out the principal similarities and differences between process theism and the idea of God developed in this book.

The concept of God proposed here shares the process view that God's relation to the temporal world consists in a succession of concrete experiences, rather than a single timeless perception. It, too, conceives God's experience of the world as ongoing, rather than a once-for-all affair.

It also shares with process theism the twofold analysis of God, or the "dipolar theism," described above. It conceives God as both absolute and relative, necessary and contingent, eternal and temporal, changeless and changing. It attributes one element in each pair of contrasts to the appropriate aspect of God's being—the essential divine character or the concrete divine experience.

The view of God proposed here also differs from process theism in several respects. The most important is its denial that God is ontologically dependent on the world. According to process thought, God and the world are equally necessary. God needs the world just as the world needs God. Either by itself is an abstraction. The idea of God without a world is just as meaningless and objectionable as that of a world without God. This is not to say that the world as it actually exists is necessary. But process theology insists that there must be some world or other for God to experience. In other words, the existence of this actual world is contingent but not the existence of a world as such. A husband must have a wife, for example, though not necessarily the wife he actually has. Similarly, according to process thought, God must have a world to experience, though not necessarily this particular world. Any world would do. But some world or other there must be.

The view of God proposed here sides with traditional Christianity in affirming God's ontological independence of the world. As traditionally understood, the God-world relation is asymmetrical. The world needs God for its existence. God does *not* need the world for His. He would exist whether there were a world or not. On this view, the existence of the world, not merely this actual world but any world at all, is not necessary but contingent. This concept of world-contingency allows us to affirm the traditional understanding of creation *ex nihilo*, or "out of nothing." According to this idea, God alone existed and then brought into existence a reality distinct from Himself—a reality that was at once nondivine and nevertheless good. So, the creaturely world had a beginning. It did not exist until God created it.

This discussion of God's openness also assumes another aspect of the traditional understanding of God that differs from process thought. This is the notion that God acts within the world, as well as upon it. Traditional Christian theology and process thought alike conceive of God as the Ultimate Reality, the power that constantly sustains all things, or "the ground of being," as Paul Tillich puts it.[2] But in addition to this fundamental metaphysical function, traditional Christianity also attributes to God certain activities within the course of creaturely experience. It sees certain events in world history as the effects of divine activity. Thus, while all reality testifies to the Creator, He also manifests Himself in certain specific ways. God sustains all history, but He is also at times an agent within history, interacting with finite historical agents. In particular, Christianity has always maintained that God was uniquely active in that particular strand of human history which culminated in the life, death, and resurrection of Jesus. Various events within this stream of history reflect the effects of God's direct involvement in human affairs, not merely His undergirding the entire historical process or His positive influence within all reality.

---

[2]*Systematic Theology* (3 vols.; Chicago: University of Chicago Press, 1951–1963), 1:235.

3

Creation and the Openness of God

Several aspects of the Creation story support the concept of an open reality. The most familiar of these is no doubt the divine command to refrain from eating of the tree of knowledge of good and evil (Gen. 2:16, 17). The prohibition indicates the reality of moral freedom. However, a preoccupation with moral freedom can obscure the nature and purpose of human freedom in general. So let us examine the larger phenomenon of human freedom before turning specifically to its moral dimension. The description of man as created in the image of God provides an important starting point.

No biblical description of human beings has received more theological attention than "the image of God" (Gen. 1:26, 27). During the passing centuries theologians have disagreed over what it refers to and how it was affected by the Fall. Medieval theologians typically regarded the *image* of God as the possession of certain natural powers or inherent qualities. To this was added a supernatural gift that enabled man to live in harmony with God. They identified this supernatural gift with the likeness of God. Due to sin man lost the extra gift, but the image itself remained intact. The Protestant Reformers and their followers rejected this distinction between "image" and "likeness." They identified the image as the orientation of man's will to God, which was almost entirely annihilated at the Fall.[1]

More recent theologians do not interpret the image of God with reference to some aspect or attribute of human beings. Instead, they tend to identify the image of God with man's situation or function in the world. Such an approach has considerable biblical support. Looking at the immediate context in which the expression "image of God" first appears, we find it closely related to man's dominion over the works of Creation. "Then God said, 'Let us make man in our image, after our likeness; and let them have dominion over the fish of the sea, and over the birds of the air, and over the cattle, and over all the earth, and over every creeping thing that creeps upon the earth' " (Gen. 1:26).

Reviewing the larger context of the entire chapter, we discover, as Dorothy Sayers observes, that the only thing said of God is the fact that He is the Creator.[2] These considerations suggest that the relation of man, the image of God, to Creation is not unlike that of God Himself. As God is Creator of all, so man in his appropriate sphere also functions as creator.

Apparently, then, the "image of God" refers to man's position of creative sovereignty over the world. Wolfhart Pannenberg terms it "creative mastery of existence."[3] Man did not, of course, have absolute sovereignty. The earth was still the Lord's. Man was His deputy, not His replacement. Humanity's treatment of the world was to reflect God's care and concern for His creatures. But the expression in its original context suggests that man was endowed with enormous creativity. Adam and Eve had the capacity and responsibility to continue the creative work of God Himself.

In creating man in His image and endowing him with dominion over the earth, God was, in effect, inviting man henceforth to participate with Him in the work of Creation. Or perhaps we should say that God intended to continue His creative activity

[1] William Hordern, "Man, Doctrine of," in *A Dictionary of Christian Theology*, edited by Alan Richardson (Philadelphia: The Westminster Press, 1969), p. 203.
[2] Dorothy L. Sayers, *Christian Letters to a Post-Christian World* (Grand Rapids, Michigan: William B. Eerdmans Publishing Co., 1969), pp. 100, 101.
[3] *What Is Man? Contemporary Anthropology in Christian Perspective*, translated by Duane A. Priebe (Philadelphia: Fortress Press, 1970), p. 15.

through the agency of His creatures. At any rate, Genesis 1 presents us with the God who creates a world and gives it the capacity for self-creation.

The situation was not unlike that of an artist completing a vast and intricate mural. As his climactic act he hands the brush to one of the figures in the painting with the invitation to carry on the work he had begun. Accordingly, the future of the earth was by no means closed at the end of Creation Week. It was, to the contrary, immensely open. The future was left open to any number of courses that the creatures, man in particular, should select.

The openness of Creation thus refers to the capacity of God's creatures for further creative activity. It does not imply any imperfection in God's work itself. God did not need man to make up for what He had failed to do. For as the Scripture says, "Thus the heavens and the earth were finished, and all the host of them. And on the seventh day God finished his work which he had done" (Gen. 2:1, 2). These words do not indicate that all creative activity stopped. Rather, they imply that the world now had everything it needed to fulfill God's purposes for it. One phase of the creation of the world had ended. Another was about to begin.

The self-creative quality of the earth's inhabitants is evident at other points in the Creation narrative as well. One is God's command that the creatures "be fruitful and multiply" (Gen. 1:28). God might, presumably, have created at once all the specimens of each form of life this world would ever need. But He chose to populate the earth by giving the various creatures the capacity to reproduce. In a sense, therefore, the creatures themselves participate in the work of creation.

God's invitation to Adam to name the animals also illustrates the self-creative quality of creation (Gen. 2:19, 20). In ancient thought the name bore one's identity or the essence of one's character. The changing of Jacob's name dramatically illustrates this (cf. Gen. 32:27, 28). Nothing fully existed until it received a name. Accordingly, when God invited Adam to name the animals, He was asking Adam to share in the very work of creation. It was as if God left part of creation deliberately unfinished, or open, in order for man to decide how it should be completed.

The divine command to refrain from eating of the tree of knowledge of good and evil (Gen. 2:16, 17) indicates another important way in which reality was open. A command makes sense only if the recipient is capable of doing either what is required or forbidden, in other words, only if he is a responsible being. So the divine prohibition implies that man is morally free. Adam and Eve were free to render or refuse obedience to God. Since, as we noted earlier, freedom involves the presence of genuine alternatives, God could not give man the freedom to obey and at the same time withhold the power to disobey. "Freedom to obey" is nothing if it is not also the freedom to disobey. Consequently, had man been incapable of disobedience, his fulfillment of God's requirements would not have been voluntary. And the word *moral* could not apply.

The affirmation of moral freedom requires an open view of reality. When God gave man moral freedom, He was leaving undecided whether or not man would obey. In other words, He left open man's response to God's expectations of him. God might, presumably, have constructed man to respond to Him in only one way. But in that case moral experience would have been impossible, because man would not have been responsible for his behavior. Man is a morally free being, and the content of his decision to obey or disobey must have been indefinite until man himself made the decision. Accordingly, to the extent that reality was yet to be determined by human decisions, it was open or indefinite.

The open view of reality thus finds important support in the biblical descriptions of man as a creative and morally responsible being. In creating beings who were themselves capable of "creating" and in endowing them with moral freedom, God created an open world. It was a world whose future was not fixed in advance. The future could follow different courses, depending on the decisions of God's creatures. Consequently, the future of this planet was not definite at the conclusion of Creation Week. True, a great deal of what would happen was the inevitable consequence of factors present at the outset, but not everything—not the effects of moral and creative decisions. Henceforth, the course of history would be determined, not by God alone, but by God and the creatures.

An open view of reality requires an open conception of God's relation to the world. For if God's knowledge perfectly reflects reality, and if reality is dynamic, open, and constantly developing, then the same must be true of God's knowledge. It, too, is dynamic, open, and constantly developing. The contents of God's experience, therefore, are not fixed or static. They are constantly increased as new data pass from the developing world into the mind of God. God's relation to the creaturely world is thus subtle and complex. Instead of merely acting upon the world, God also reacts to developments within the world. The influence between God and the world flows both ways. God not only affects the world, but the world also affects Him.

God's experience of the world is open and dynamic, we have argued, and His knowledge of the world is constantly increasing. This raises an interesting question. If God's knowledge of us is constantly increasing, was there a time when God knew nothing? If God needs the world in order to know anything, and if the world had a beginning, it seems, the answer must be "Yes; before the creation of the world God knew nothing, for there was nothing for Him to experience." But this is unacceptable. The notion of a totally ignorant being of any sort is highly questionable, and in the case of God it is absurd. A "totally ignorant God" strikes us as a contradiction in terms. God cannot exist without some sort of knowledge or experience. This is why some philosophers insist that the world must be just as eternal as God is: because without a world there would be nothing for God to experience. But this position is unacceptable, too. It makes God just as dependent on the world as the world is on God, and such a view conflicts with the biblical doctrine of creation.

The problem with this line of thought is the assumption that God needs the world in order to know something, or that God would have nothing to experience unless the creaturely world existed. It is true that God's knowledge *of the world* depends on the world, but it does not follow that God would have nothing to know without a world to experience. There remains the possibility of divine self-knowledge, the idea that God experienced himself before He created the world. It may be difficult for us to imagine such an experience, but this alone does not invalidate the concept. In fact, it finds support in the Christian understanding of God as a threefold being.

The doctrine of the Trinity is an important aspect of the Christian understanding of God. The idea of the Trinity expresses the fundamental conviction that God's inner life, or His very nature, reflects the distinctions between Father, Son, and Holy Spirit that we see in the history of salvation. In other words, God has never been sheer undifferentiated unity; He has always existed in three persons. These words of Jesus support this idea: "Father, I desire that they . . . behold my glory which thou has given me in thy love for me before the foundation of the world" (John 17:24). The concept of the Trinity allows—in fact, it requires—a dynamic understanding of God as He is in himself, quite apart from the creaturely world. And on this basis we can speak of God as having relationships and enjoying experiences before the world existed.

The biblical writers describe God's sensitivity to the creaturely world in an impressive variety of ways. God is completely aware of all that happens. He discerns the most apparently insignificant event. Jesus assured His disciples of God's care for them by saying that God notices when a sparrow falls and numbers the hairs of our heads (Matt. 10:29, 30).

God is not only aware of everything in the creaturely world, but He also responds to events in different ways. According to Genesis, for example, when He views the extreme wickedness of the antediluvians, "the Lord was sorry that he had made man on the earth, and it grieved him to his heart" (Gen. 6:6). In contrast, according to Jesus' most famous parables, God rejoices when sinners repent, just as men and women rejoice at the recovery of something lost. "There will be more joy in heaven over one sinner who repents than over ninety-nine righteous persons who need no repentance" (Luke 15:7).

God's concern for the sin and suffering of human beings finds poignant expression in the writings of the Hebrew prophets. God is outraged when the poor are mistreated:

Hear this word, you cows of Bashan, who are in the moun-

tain of Samaria, who oppress the poor, who crush the needy. . . .
The Lord God has sworn by his holiness that, behold, the days
are coming upon you, when they shall take you away with hooks,
even the last of you with fishhooks (Amos 4:1, 2).

Hear, you heads of Jacob and rulers of the house of Israel! Is
it not for you to know justice?—you who hate the good and love
the evil, who tear the skin from off my people, and their flesh
from off their bones. . . . Then they will cry to the Lord, but he
will not answer them; he will hide his face from them at that
time, because they have made their deeds evil (Mic. 3:1–4).

The prophets describe God's attitudes toward the people of
Israel as the feelings prevalent in the closest human relationships. God feels like a spurned husband. He yearns for the return of His beloved people:

Surely, as a faithless wife leaves her husband, so have you
been faithless to me, O house of Israel, says the Lord (Jer. 3:20).

And I will punish her for the feast days of the Baals when
she burned incense to them and decked herself with her ring
and jewelry, and went after her lovers, and forgot me, says the
Lord.

Therefore, behold, I will allure her, and bring her into the
wilderness, and speak tenderly to her (Hos. 2:13, 14).

The tenderness of God's concern for His people both resembles and surpasses that of parents for their children:

Is Ephraim my dear son? Is he my darling child? For as often
as I speak against him, I do remember him still. Therefore my
heart yearns for him; I will surely have mercy on him, says the
Lord (Jer. 31:20).

When Israel was a child, I loved him, and out of Egypt I
called my son. . . . It was I who taught Ephraim to walk, I took
them up in my arms (Hos. 11:1–3).

Can a woman forget her sucking child, that she should have
no compassion on the son of her womb? Even these may forget,
yet I will not forget you. Behold, I have graven you on the palms
of my hands; your walls are continually before me (Isa. 49:15,
16).

The picture of God that emerges from these representative
passages, and from the Bible as a whole, is not that of a being
who has the whole value of creaturely reality in the isolation of
a single timeless perception. God is by no means the detached
observer. He is not unmoved by the course of human history.

The Bible portrays God as a person who is infinitely concerned with and sensitive to every aspect of the world. He responds to events as they actually happen. Sometimes He rejoices (Luke 15:7). Sometimes He sorrows (Gen. 6:6). Sometimes He wishes that things were drastically different than they are. His various reactions to events are genuine. They are not merely apparent. In a word, God is *open* to the world of creaturely experience. He is truly affected by our decisions, achievements, and disappointments.

This view suggests an intimate relation between God and the individual person. It implies that God shares the events of a person's life as he experiences them. God appreciates the full reality of one's joy or sorrow at the precise time that person experiences it. It is not a datum in His knowledge from all eternity. My experience here and now contributes something novel to God's experience too. This is impossible according to the usual view. For God possesses in one timeless perception the full value of all reality—past and future. The actual experiences of individual human beings contribute nothing to God's experience that He does not already have.

There is another quality of experience, excluded by the traditional view of God's relation to the world, that the open view makes it possible to attribute to God. This is the capacity for risk. A risk is an undertaking whose outcome is indefinite. The person who risks his life, for example, places himself in a situation where his survival is genuinely in doubt. So, I did not risk my life when I jumped into three feet of water to save my son several years ago, because my life was in no way threatened. I fully expected to survive. We often think of love as involving a risk. There is first of all the risk that love will not be returned. And if it is, there is the risk that something harmful may befall the object of one's love. The willingness to accept the risk of being hurt or rejected is an essential aspect of our experience of love.

The open view of God allows us to attribute risk to the divine experience, thus enriching our appreciation of His love for us. There are at least two significant points in which we can think of God as assuming a risk. One is the Creation. The other in the Incarnation.

In creating morally free beings, God left the future of the world partially indefinite. Their free decisions would complete the future. In particular, God left up to human beings the decision of whether or not they would remain loyal to Him (Gen. 2:16, 17). In so doing, God undertook the risk of their disobedience. It was a risk He was willing to take, because without it their obedience would not have manifested personal love for Him.

Again at the Incarnation God undertook the risk that His Son would fail in His struggle with temptation. We can only speculate as to what the consequences of that possibility would have been. Perhaps they are literally unimaginable to us. But the genuineness of Christ's temptations strongly supports the reality of the risk that God assumed (Matt. 4:1–11; 26:36–44; Luke 4:1–13; 22:39–44; Heb. 2:18; 4:15). And this heightens, if anything, our appreciation of His love. In giving His Son for man's salvation, God was not merely expressing His disposition toward humanity. He was also running the risk of permanently disastrous consequences to the Godhead itself.

The customary view, however, of God's relation to time makes it impossible to speak of God as ever risking anything. If God could foresee from all eternity the fall of man and the success of salvation, then neither Creation nor the Incarnation really involved a genuine risk. If at Creation God knew with absolute certainty that man would fall, He was not risking the moral harmony of the universe in making man. He was simply sacrificing it. Similarly, if God knew with complete certainty that Christ's earthly mission would end in victory, He did not risk His Son in sending Him to the world for man's salvation. He simply paid the price for a guaranteed result.

Of course, to deny God's capacity for risk does not wholly deny His love. But it does exclude a quality from His experience that is one of the most moving aspects of human love, namely, the willingness to commit oneself wholly to another in spite of an uncertain and indefinite future. The open view of God makes this exclusion unnecessary.

Besides rendering faithfully the biblical description of God, the open view of God's relation to the world makes possible a coherent conception of God's motive for creating as well as of the divine decision to create. God's motive for creating is noto-riously obscure, as John Calvin and others have cogently ob-served.[4] But Christian theology traditionally attributes God's cre-ative activity to His transcendent love—a love that seeks fellowship and expression. God brings the world into existence because He desires the happiness of its inhabitants (see Gen. 1:28; Isa. 45:18). God creates out of a desire to give. He does not create out of a desire to meet His own needs, as if He were somehow inwardly compelled to create or would remain incom-plete without a world to rule.

The crucial question, though, is whether the actual existence of the creaturely world contributes anything to God's experi-ence. According to the view of absolute foreknowledge, it does not. For if God sees the world in all its reality before Creation, then He gains no new satisfaction from its actual, as opposed to imagined, existence. He has all the value of any world simply by foreseeing it.

By attributing temporal experiences to God, the open view of God's relation to the world provides for a coherent conception of divine decision. On the view that God's knowledge of the future is absolute and all-inclusive, there is no possibility of "de-cision" on God's part. After all, no aspect of the future is indef-inite to Him, including His own activities. Knowing the entire course of the future, God also knows the content of all His de-cisions. But to know exactly what one will decide is nothing other than to have made the decision already. Nothing is left to be decided. Indeed, since the very meaning of "decision" implies a transition from "undecided" to "decided" and thus requires a temporal distinction, the concept of "divine decision" is inher-ently contradictory according to the conventional view. If, how-ever, God's experience is sequential in some sense, then we can think of God as really making decisions, as choosing between

---

[4]Calvin urges Christians not to go behind God's act of creation in their specu-lation (*Institutes of Christian Religion*, I.14.1). A contemporary philosopher of religion, James F. Ross, describes the divine motivation for Creation as a paradox (*Introduction to the Philosophy of Religion* [New York: The Macmillan Company, 1969], p. 65).

alternatives, as making definite something that was previously indefinite. Moreover, we can distinguish among three things that the customary view confuses: God's envisionment of reality, God's decision to create, and God's experience of the actual world.

4

Evil and the Openness of God

The view that God's experience is open has another advantage. It makes possible an effective response to the problem of evil. The reality of evil is both the strongest obstacle to personal faith in God and the most formidable intellectual challenge to theism. How can one reconcile the existence of evil in the world with the qualities of love and omnipotence attributed to God in the Judeo-Christian tradition? To quote David Hume's trenchant formulation: "Is he willing to prevent evil, but not able? then is he impotent. Is he able, but not willing? then is he malevolent. Is he both able and willing? whence then is evil?"[1]

The classic response to this challenge begins at least as far back as Augustine. It is called the free will defense. The free will defense insists that evil did not originate with God but with the decisions of certain created beings. By misusing their freedom they rebelled against God's authority.

Alvin Plantinga, a contemporary philosopher, summarizes the free will defense in this way.

A world containing creatures who are significantly free (and freely perform more good than evil actions) is more valuable, all

---

[1] Dialogues Concerning Natural Religion, Part 10 (*The English Philosophers From Bacon to Mill*, edited by Edwin A. Burtt [New York: The Modern Library, 1939], p. 741).

else being equal, than a world containing no free creatures at all. Now God can create free creatures, but He can't *cause* or *determine* them to do only what is right. For if He does so, then they aren't significantly free after all; they do not do what is right *freely*. To create creatures capable of *moral good*, therefore, He must create creatures capable of moral evil; and He can't give these creatures the freedom to perform evil and at the same time prevent them from doing so. As it turned out, sadly enough, some of the free creatures God created went wrong in the exercise of their freedom; this is the source of moral evil. The fact that free creatures sometimes go wrong, however, counts neither against God's omnipotence nor against His goodness; for He could have forestalled the occurrence of moral evil only by removing the possibility of moral good.[2]

The free will defense relieves God of responsibility for evil only if the existence of evil was a mere possibility, not an actuality, with the creation of morally free beings. It fails if the eventual existence of evil was definite at the time of Creation. For in that case, God created a world in which evil *would*, rather than *could*, exist. And only if God created a world where evil merely *could* exist—where its existence was possible but not definite—is it the case that God is not responsible for evil. The alternative is a world in which the emergence of evil is definite. In such a case evil would represent an integral part of the scheme of things. In other words, God created an evil world simply by creating a world at all. But if this is the case, evil turns out not to be evil after all. That is, it is no longer an intruder. It somehow belongs.

Perhaps it should not surprise us that a number have taken this alternative position in response to the problem of evil. In his book *Evil and the God of Love*, for example, John Hick argues that evil plays an important role in the fulfillment of God's purposes for the world. Therefore, God envisioned it from the beginning.[3] Specifically, evil contributes to the process of "soul-making." It enables human beings to develop certain traits of character that would have been impossible in a completely untainted environment. Attributes such as courage, compassion,

---

[2]*God, Freedom and Evil* (New York: Harper Torchbooks, 1974), p. 30.
[3]Hick outlines his "vale of soul-making" theodicy in *Evil and the God of Love* (rev. ed.; New York: Harper & Row, Publishers, 1978), pp. 253–261.

and penitence are inconceivable in a perfect world. So the presence of evil and its effects make an essential contribution to the realization of God's objectives for human life.

John Hick rejects the free will defense, or "Augustinian theodicy," as he calls it. He favors an "Irenaean theodicy" for two basic reasons. First, he finds the traditional idea of the Fall totally incomprehensible. He cannot conceive that a completely innocent being, perfectly oriented to the service of God, should abruptly and without cause rebel against God.[4] Second, proponents of the free will defense usually attribute absolute foreknowledge to God. This in effect, Hick argues, makes God ultimately responsible for evil anyway.[5] For his part, Hick prefers to attribute responsibility for evil to God from the outset. Then he can try to find out the role God intended it to play.

Hick's objection to the concept of the Fall is not convincing. The incomprehensibility of the Fall is precisely the point proponents of the free will defense wish to make. If the original nature of the creatures provided any explanation for the Fall, then the Creator would be ultimately responsible for evil. This is just what the free will defense seeks to avoid. Hick is correct, however, in observing that the free will defense fails if we attribute absolute foreknowledge to God.

The concept of absolute divine foreknowledge renders ineffective the free will defense. In the final analysis it makes God ultimately responsible for evil for the following reasons: If God knows the future absolutely, then He went ahead with Creation while knowing full well that evil would enter the universe. Someone may argue that the eventual entrance of evil into a morally free universe is inevitable. Evil is simply the price of a universe where beings are genuinely free. But if this is true, then God is clearly responsible for the existence of evil by virtue of His decision to create morally free beings.

---

[4]Hick reiterates this fundamental objection throughout his discussion (pp. 62, 63, 66, 174, 250, 251, 332).

[5]According to Hick, the Augustinian tradition wraps "the incomprehensible conception of the self-creation of evil *ex nihilo* in a further mystery, which, without rendering the first any less mysterious, largely nullifies it as a refuge for theodicy by casting upon God the more ultimate responsibility for the creation of beings who He knew would, if created, freely sin" (p. 66).

Others may argue, not that evil is the inevitable consequence of moral freedom, but that evil was the eventual choice of certain morally free beings. They, therefore, not God, are responsible for evil. According to this reasoning, God foresaw the existence of evil because He knew what their future moral choices would be.

However, this argument does not make God any less responsible for the existence of evil. If anything, in fact, it makes Him even more responsible. It provides Him with the perfect means of eliminating all risk of evil while creating a universe where moral good is possible. For if God could foresee infallibly every future event and every future decision, then He must have known in advance which creatures would remain loyal to Him and which would disobey. Consequently, God could have prevented evil simply by creating beings whom He foreknew would always choose the good. The world would thus have been populated with morally free beings who would never, God knows, misuse their freedom to reject His authority. There could have been both creaturely freedom and complete moral security.

Defenders of absolute foreknowledge may rebut this criticism in two ways. But in each case the rebuttal rests on a presupposition that is incompatible with the classical concept of divine foreknowledge. One is to argue that it would be "unfair" of God to populate the universe exclusively with loyal creatures. This would amount to "stacking the deck" in His own favor. The other is to maintain that a universe populated with loyal beings alone would not be free. Freedom requires options, and a universe where disloyalty is not one of the options is not really free. Therefore God was obligated to create beings whom He foreknew would rebel as well as beings whom He foreknew would be loyal.

This line of thought is flawed in several ways. In the first place, it confuses freedom with the actualization of certain options. But all that freedom requires is the availability of certain options. A universe whose inhabitants could rebel if they chose is one where freedom is real. It is not necessary that they actually do so.

The same line of reasoning also makes evil inevitable in a

world where freedom exists. For if the creation of beings whose rebellion God foreknew was necessary for genuine freedom, then God created a world in which evil plays an essential role. Evil is not an inexplicable intruder in the drama of creation. Rather, it is an indispensable member of the cast.

Of those who object that God is not fair unless He creates rebels as well as loyal subjects, we must ask, "Unfair to whom?" to Himself? or to the loyal creatures? Hardly. The absence of evil deprives them of nothing beneficial. Is it then somehow unfair to the evildoers themselves, who are never created? If so, we face a host of perplexing questions. How, for example, can non-existent beings be the victims of unfair treatment? Indeed, unless and until they exist, how can they be treated at all, fairly or otherwise? But suppose their envisionment in the mind of God gives them some sort of reality. The question now is, when did they acquire this status of "going-to-exist"? When was their existence definite? Presumably, when God decided to create them. But that leaves us with the conclusion that God decided to create beings who would do evil. And this makes God responsible for evil.

There seems, then, to be no way to avoid making God responsible for evil if we accept the usual view of God's relation to time. Hick is correct in arguing that absolute foreknowledge renders the free will defense ineffective. But we do not have to abandon the free will defense for this reason. We can revise our concept of God's relation to the world. The open view of God and reality makes it possible to affirm the free will defense and thus to relieve God of any responsibility for evil.

The view that future free decisions are indefinite until they occur and are therefore in principle unknowable in advance gives us the following scenario. God decided to create a world containing morally free beings. These beings had the choice of serving Him or not. Since their obedience or disobedience was something He left up to them to decide, it was not definite. Therefore their future decision was not knowable until they existed and made the choice themselves. God knew they *could* rebel when he created them. But it was not certain that they *would* rebel until they decided to do so. Thus, God is responsible only for the possibility of evil (simply because He created morally free beings). But He is not responsible for the actuality of evil. The creatures are entirely to blame for that.

The open view of God's relation to the world is thus superior to the more conventional view in several important ways. By maintaining that "time is real for God," we are able to affirm genuine creaturely freedom. This, in turn, provides a coherent response to the problem of evil. With the open view of God's relation to the world, we can also conceive of God's love as involving moment-by-moment sensitivity to the experiences of His creatures, and we can also think of Him as accepting risks on their behalf. Both these conceptions the familiar view excludes.

Thus far in our discussion we have seen why we need an open view of God. We have also discussed what this concept basically involves. We observed that the open view makes more sense in light of our fundamental intuitions about reality. It also renders more accurately than the traditional view some important biblical descriptions of God and man. We are now in a position to explore more fully the theological value of this view.

The openness of God is more than a defensible interpretation of God's relation to the world. It has important implications for the concepts of divine foreknowledge, providence, prophecy, and predestination. The open view of God requires a revisionary interpretation of each of these ideas, but in every case this revision enhances and enriches the concept involved.

The open view of God therefore is not merely acceptable. It is profoundly suggestive. It provides a new perspective on the doctrine of God as a whole, which is both theologically important and experientially helpful. Let us begin with the most obvious question raised by the openness of God. What is God's relation to the future, if indeed it is not that of absolute foreknowledge?

5

The Future and the Openness of God

One way to express the basic difference between the usual view of God's relation to the world and the alternative this book proposes is to say that they involve contrasting concepts of the future. The customary view states that God knows the future in all its detail. It implies that the future itself is there to be known—fixed and changeless in every respect. We have seen that such a concept excludes creaturely freedom because genuine freedom requires that part of the future be indefinite until decided by free personal agents. In order to affirm creaturely freedom, the open view of God maintains that certain aspects of the future are as yet indefinite. Therefore they are unknowable. And this means that God's knowledge of the future cannot be exhaustive.

Two misgivings may arise from the idea that God does not enjoy exhaustive knowledge of the future. One is the belief that God's knowledge is less than perfect if there is anything He does not know. The other is the fear that a God ignorant of the future cannot meet its challenges. Neither objection is well-founded.

The belief that God does not know the content of future decisions compromises the perfection of His knowledge only if we regard these decisions as there to be known before they are actually made. But this is precisely what the open view of God denies. Future free decisions do not exist in any sense before they are made. So the real difference between the traditional view of God and the alternative proposed here is not that one attributes perfect knowledge to God, while the other doesn't. Both affirm that God knows everything there is to know. They differ, however, in their concepts of what there is to know. In particular, they differ in their concepts of the future. If, as the familiar view maintains, the future is already there in all its detail, then God knows everything that will ever happen. But if future free decisions do not yet exist, they are not there to be known until they are made. And the fact that God does not know them ahead of time represents no deficiency in His knowledge. Not knowing that which isn't there to be known hardly constitutes ignorance. Just as not seeing what is not there to see is not a kind of blindness.

The consensus of Christian thinkers ranging from Thomas Aquinas to C. S. Lewis is that omnipotence, or perfect power, does not mean simply that God can do anything.[1] We cannot put just any combination of words after the expression "God can" and make a coherent statement. We cannot say, for example, that God can make a square circle or add two and two and get five or make a rock so big that He cannot lift it. This does not mean that there is something that God cannot do. Making square circles and the like is not doing something. It is literally nonsense. It implies no deficiency in divine power to say that God cannot do the logically impossible, not because the logically impossible lies beyond God's power but because it is not anything "doable."

The point with respect to divine foreknowledge is precisely the same. Perfect knowledge, or omniscience, is not simply "knowing everything." Rather, it is "knowing everything there is to know." And, as we have seen, future free decisions are not there to be known until they are actually made. Accordingly, God's not knowing them in advance does not imply that His knowledge is less than perfect. It simply means that His knowl-

---

[1] " 'Nothing which implies contradiction falls under the omnipotence of God' " (Thomas Aquinas, *Summa Theologica*, la, Question 25, Article 4, quoted in C. S. Lewis, *The Problem of Pain* [New York: The Macmillan Company, 1962], p. 26). According to Lewis himself, "Omnipotence means power to do all that is intrinsically possible, not to do the intrinsically impossible" (*Ibid.*, p. 28).

edge corresponds precisely with what there is to know.

The recognition that God's knowledge reflects perfectly all there is to know prevents us from concluding that He is utterly ignorant of the future, just as it prevents us from affirming absolute foreknowledge. The difference between the past and the future is not that the past is wholly definite, while the future is wholly indefinite. The difference is that whereas the past is entirely definite, the future is only partially definite. Therefore the future is to some extent open. As the perfect reflection of reality, God's knowledge of the past is exhaustive. It is the infallible register of all that has ever happened. But He knows the future as definite only to the extent that the course of future events is already determined. It is indefinite from His perspective to the extent that it is yet to be decided. So, the fact that God does not know the future in all its detail does not mean that He is utterly ignorant of what will happen. Neither does it reduce His relation to the future to sheer guesswork. It simply means that His knowledge of the future differs from His knowledge of the past, because the future and the past are distinguished by two different degrees of definiteness.

The open view of God is therefore entirely compatible with the view that God knows a great deal about the future course of events. Certainly some of what will happen in the future is determined by factors that already exist. This forms the basic presupposition for all scientific endeavor. In fact, the vast majority of future events may be the inevitable outworking of past and present causes. All that our open view of reality requires is that the future be indefinite to the extent that the world contains genuine freedom. And the openness that genuine freedom entails may actually constitute a small proportion of what will happen. Possessing exhaustive knowledge of the past, God therefore knows all that will happen as the result of factors already in existence. In other words, God knows infallibly (or foreknows absolutely) all the future consequences of the past and present.

God's future thus resembles ours in that it is both definite and indefinite. But it differs greatly from ours in the extent to which it is definite. Since we are largely ignorant of the past and present, the future appears vastly indefinite to us. We know very little of what will happen because we know and understand so little of what has already happened. God, in contrast, knows all that has happened. Therefore a great deal of the future that appears vague and indefinite to us must be vividly clear to Him.

Besides the future consequences of past and present causes, God may also foresee as definite some of His own actions. This would include divine actions that are not dependent upon circumstances in the creaturely world but arise solely from God's personal decision. God's original creative activity offers an example (hypothetical to some) of such an action (see Job 38:4–7; Ps. 33:6–9; 102:25). Having decided to create, God would have foreseen His creative activity as something definite, since nothing could conceivably interfere with the fulfillment of His plan. In this respect, too, the future for us is radically different. For we cannot be certain that any of our plans will be fulfilled. Our power to accomplish our purposes always remains limited. We have no control over the many things that could prevent their fulfillment.

Moreover, all our future actions depend on our being alive, and this is by no means assured. Unlike God, our existence is radically contingent. It depends on a variety of factors (Ps. 90:5, 6; 103:15, 16). But His existence could never end (Ps. 90:2, 4; 93:2; 102:27; 1 Tim. 6:16). Thus, the definiteness of some of God's actions reflects the vast difference between divine and creaturely status in the universe. In a personal sense, the future is almost entirely indefinite for us and only partly indefinite for Him.

Not only does a great deal of the future that is indefinite from our standpoint appear definite to God, but even where the future must be indefinite from God's perspective (as in the case of free creaturely decisions), it appears drastically different to God than to us. This is because God knows each human being intimately, as the Bible frequently indicates (1 Sam. 16:7; Ps. 94:11; 139:2–4; Matt. 10:30; Heb. 4:2). He knows the precise range of alternatives available to every individual.

A number of factors determine the range of options available to a person. The most basic of these is man's specific form of creaturely existence, his essential human nature. A human being does not have the option, for example, of living without oxygen.

His physical constitution will not permit it. So his choice of environment is limited to the earth's atmosphere or to some reproduction of it.

A person's choices are also limited by his unique individuality; those characteristics that distinguish him from other human beings. My lack of size and speed, for example, prevents me from pursuing a career in professional football. Similarly, the absence of musical talent rules out my singing for the Metropolitan Opera. And my ancestry precludes my becoming king of England.

A person's previous decisions and experiences further restrict the range of options available to him. Having decided in college to study theology rather than medicine, I do not now have the choice of practicing either radiology or surgery. My previous decision excludes those particular options.

Because of such factors, no human being enjoys unrestricted freedom. In every situation his options are limited. And God knows exactly what these options are for every individual in every situation. In addition, knowing each individual intimately as He does, God also knows which of the available options a person will likely select. Consequently, while the future is open for God, to the extent that there is genuine personal freedom, it is not "wide open." Although the future is not absolutely foreknowable, it is not wildly unpredictable either. Every finite choice falls within a limited range of options whose perimeter God knows precisely.

In addition to the precise range of options available to His creatures and the likely choices they will make, God is also aware of His own potential responses to each creaturely decision. He can envision a course of action appropriate to every conceivable situation (see Jer. 18:7–10). So there is no possibility of God's being caught by surprise by any development in the creaturely world. He will never find Himself at a loss to meet a situation. As we shall see in the next chapter, this enables God to maintain ultimate sovereignty over the world, even though His control over the actual course of events is not absolute since it allows for creaturely freedom.

In light of these considerations, we can see that the open view of God does not render God helpless before a dark and mysterious future. Nothing can happen that He has not already envisioned and for which He has not made adequate preparation. Consequently, although God does not know the future absolutely, He nevertheless anticipates it perfectly. He faces the future with complete foresight.

Perfect anticipation consists in knowing what *will* happen (or cannot but happen) and what you will do to respond to what happens. It also involves knowing what *might* happen or what you should do in response to that. But it does not consist in knowing everything that actually will happen.

A hiker, for example, who prepares perfectly for a trip through the High Sierras will take adequate food and bedding, since he will obviously have to eat and sleep. He will also take weatherproof gear and certain medical supplies, since he knows what might happen during his trek. If his anticipation is perfect (which is impossible on a human level, of course), nothing can happen for which he has not made adequate preparation, even though he does not know ahead of time everything that will actually occur.

Now, God knows exactly what will happen in the future as the inevitable consequence of past and present factors in reality. He also knows exactly what some of His own future actions will be. So part of the future is already definite from God's point of view. In addition, however, God also knows what could happen as the result of future creaturely decisions. And He knows just what course of action He will take in response to each eventuality. Taking these factors together, we can see that the future is not at all wide open as far as God is concerned. Neither is it entirely closed. Instead, it is open—to the extent that it is yet to be determined by creaturely decisions and God's responses to them.

It is interesting and important to notice that the effects of absolute foreknowledge and perfect anticipation will be strikingly similar in certain respects. But the two concepts are significantly different.

Returning to the High Sierras illustration, let us imagine two hikers on a seven-day trek. One is vastly experienced. The other is on his first backpacking trip. Suppose, for illustration, that the expert has perfectly anticipated the trip. The first day it rains. The expert pitches a waterproof tent, and the two sit out the storm. The next day the novice suffers a snakebite. The expert calmly applies a tourniquet and administers an injection of antivenin serum. Thereafter a bear attacks them, and the expert dispatches it with his high-powered rifle. The novice breaks his leg, which the expert, an orthopedic surgeon, carefully sets. Finally the two are rescued from an avalanche by a helicopter that the expert summons with his portable radio transmitter.

So adequate is the expert's response to every situation that the novice may suspect that he knew before the trip began everything that would happen. Maybe the expert had staged the various episodes himself. Neither, however, is logically required. The complete adequacy of the expert's response testifies to his perfect preparation for the trip, which includes an awareness of all that could happen, but not necessarily to an advance knowledge of what actually would happen. In other words, the expert's preparation is adequately accounted for by perfect anticipation. Absolute foreknowledge is not required.

Similarly, the conceivable effects of absolute foreknowledge and perfect divine anticipation may be identical. In either case, God's response to the course of events in the creaturely world will appear to be exactly right. Everything He does seems to be ideally suited to the circumstances. But a world of difference exists between the two with respect to creaturely freedom. Genuine freedom is wholly compatible with the concept of perfect anticipation. But absolute foreknowledge, however construed, utterly excludes freedom.

The open view of God, then, views the future as partly definite and partly indefinite from God's perspective. His relation to the future is one of perfect anticipation. This understanding allows for creaturely freedom. But it does more. The partial openness of the future also calls for the dynamic interaction between God and the creaturely world. We can no longer think of Him as a detached observer. God does not watch impassively while history inexorably unfolds. Instead, we must now regard Him as an active participant in the ongoing course of events. And this brings us to a new conception of divine providence.

6

Providence and the Openness of God

The concept of providence encompasses a broad range of ideas. On the most general level, the term refers to God's continued activity in the world He has created. He guides it toward the fulfillment of His purposes. God's ongoing involvement in the world includes the support of the natural order. "Thou hast made heaven, the heaven of heavens, with all their host, the earth and all that is on it, the seas and all that is in them; and thou preservest all of them" (Neh. 9:6).

From a theological perspective the so-called laws of nature simply describe God's customary mode of action in the world. They are not ironclad rules by which He is bound. According to traditional Christianity, God occasionally departs from His familiar pattern of operations. We call such events miracles. Miracles are manifestations of divine power for which we can find no adequate naturalistic explanation. The resurrection of Jesus, for example, is clearly a miracle. No natural force could restore life to the dead. Only direct divine intervention in the ordinary course of things could accomplish that (Rom. 4:17).

In addition to the general concept of God's ongoing involvement in the world, providence is also more narrowly understood as God's involvement in the course of human history. In contrast to miracles, providence in this sense is more restricted. Here providence consists of events that are capable of natural explanation on one level. However, to the eye of faith they represent the fulfillment of God's plan.

Luke's account of the location of Jesus' birth may illustrate God's use of human actions and decisions to achieve His ends (Luke 2:1–7). The decree that brought Mary and Joseph to Bethlehem was issued by the Roman emperor. So on one level, Jesus' birth in Bethlehem resulted from the decree of Caesar Augustus. From another perspective, however, His birth there fulfilled the famous prophecy of Micah 5:2 that foretold the Messiah's birthplace (see Matt. 2:1–6). God providentially employed the imperial decree to help fulfill this aspect of His plan for Jesus' life.

The Bible often speaks of God as using unpleasant experiences to achieve His purposes. In his emotional reunion with his brothers, Joseph interpreted their treacherous treatment of him years before as God's way of ensuring their survival. According to Genesis, he said to them: "And now do not be distressed, or angry with yourselves, because you sold me here; for God sent me before you to preserve life. . . . And God sent me before you to preserve for you a remnant on earth, and to keep alive for you many survivors. So it was not you who sent me here, but God" (Gen. 45:5–8).

The most striking manifestations of providence occur when God responds to events that to all appearances will thwart His purposes but in actuality end up promoting His intentions. Pharaoh's reluctance to release the Israelites seemed to prevent the fulfillment of God's plan for the chosen people. But in the long run Pharaoh's stubbornness heightened the drama of their deliverance (Ex. 5:1—15:21). The Crucifixion is the outstanding New Testament manifestation of divine providence. At first, Jesus' death appeared to abort His mission and negate its divine authority. However, the cross emerges as the supreme moment in salvation history (compare Gal. 3:13 and 2 Cor. 5:21). Providential power turned an instrument of torture and humiliation into the symbol of love and salvation. God used the treachery and ingratitude of men in a way that accentuates the magnitude of His love and self-sacrifice.

The view that reality is open rather than closed and that God's experience of the temporal world is dynamic rather than static requires a more subtle understanding of divine providence than the more traditional notions call for. The usual view of fore-knowledge assumes that God exhaustively knows the future. It implies that providential activity is simply the outworking of a plan, complete in all its details, that God formulated once and for all in the remote past. God knows all that would ever occur, including every human action and decision. Therefore He could establish an invariant pattern of operations from which the course of events has never deviated. Accordingly, His present activity could consist in merely observing this plan unfold.

According to the view that reality is open, however, this relatively passive divine attitude toward human history is inconceivable. The actual course of events is not completely perceptible to God in advance. Rather, it becomes apparent to Him as the participants contribute their individual decisions and actions. Consequently, God must respond to situations in the world as they develop. In this way He implements His plans and accomplishes His purposes. The open view of reality requires a complex interaction between God and the temporal world.

The open view of God does not regard God's "plan" for this world as fixed or invariant from eternity. Rather, God's purpose must be implemented in a dynamic historical context. Therefore it is constantly modified in response to creaturely behavior. And God's actions within the world are not simply the recital of a preestablished role. They are in part reactions to the decisions of other individuals. In short, God must "improvise" as circumstances change if He wishes to reach His objectives. This does not mean that God lacks a plan and simply has to make do. Instead, it means that God's plans must be sufficiently comprehensive and flexible to include a variety of possible courses of action.

Consequently, when we speak of God's plans from the open view of reality, we need to distinguish between (1) God's ultimate objectives for the world and (2) the course, or courses, of action that He undertakes in order to reach them. We cannot collapse the two, as the customary view of God's relation to the world often seems to do. The importance of this distinction becomes evident when we consider the most general plan of all—God's plan for humanity.

Presumably God's ultimate objective for the human race consisted in the eventual population of this planet with morally free and intelligent beings. He desired them to live in harmonious fellowship with one another. He wanted them to be united in supreme devotion to Him. Such a world contained the possibility of rebellion. Moral freedom, as we have already observed, consists in the power to give or withhold allegiance to God. Ideally, of course, human beings would have used their freedom to render God uninterrupted obedience. This is, no doubt, what God originally intended. But in giving them freedom He certainly foresaw the possibility of sin. In light of this possibility God formulated an appropriate course of action. He would implement it in the event that sin arose (see Gen. 3:15). We generally describe this response to sin as "the plan of salvation." It included the incarnation and sacrificial death of the Son of God (John 3:14; Acts 2:23). And the purpose of the plan is to ensure the fulfillment of God's original objective for humanity, in spite of the emergence of sin in human history (John 3:16; Rom. 5:15–19).

The plan of salvation thus represents an aspect of God's original, comprehensive preparation for human life. God *formulated* this plan in view of the possibility of sin. He *implemented* it in response to the actuality of sin. The original formulation of the plan from "the foundation of the world" (1 Pet. 1:20) does not necessarily imply that the intrusion of sin in human affairs was a foregone conclusion. It only means that God had perfectly prepared for every possible development, including this most unfortunate one.

The view that God creatively responds to events as they happen entails a very high concept of divine power. The comparatively mechanical view of providence does not need such a high concept. It talks in terms of the outworking of a plan based on absolute foreknowledge. And thus it implies a plan fixed from eternity in all its details. A couple of illustrations may help make this clear.

Imagine a football coach who has copies of his opponent's play book and game plan before an important contest. Let us also imagine that during the game he can hear every play called by the opposing coach or quarterback. He can also relay the signal to his own players on the field. We would naturally expect a coach in this situation to win the game, assuming that he had relatively competent players.

Next, imagine a coach who has no advance knowledge of every play that will be called. However, he so thoroughly prepares his team for a game that they completely overwhelm the opposition. His players are ready for every conceivable formation. His defense throws every run for a loss. It intercepts every pass. His offense scores with every possession. And his special team players return all punts and kickoffs for touchdowns.

Quite obviously, the second of these coaches exhibits the greater skill. He deserves the greater admiration. He may have lacked absolute foreknowledge of the other team's plays. Nevertheless he anticipated the game perfectly and prepared his team for certain victory.

The concept that God is momentarily sensitive to the experiences of His creatures and actively involved in the course of events may raise questions about His ultimate sovereignty over history. If history is not under God's absolute control, what assurance do we have that He will ultimately prevail? How can we be confident of the triumph of God's will and the final eradication of sin?

In the previous chapter we saw that the open view of God does not require a future that is wildly unpredictable, even though it is not absolutely foreknowable. Genuine freedom requires only that the future be open *to some extent*. Moral freedom in particular requires that the ultimate allegiance of certain creatures to God be undetermined. Consequently, freedom is compatible with a limited range of options. It does not imply the absence of all restrictions. The situation is similar in the case of providence. God may not exercise absolute control over the course of history. However, this does not mean that its eventual outcome remains in doubt.

There are two bases for affirming God's ultimate sovereignty over a world whose future is genuinely open. One is God's capacity to anticipate perfectly the course of creaturely events. We analyzed this in Chapter 6. As their Creator, God knows the range of options available to His creatures. And since He knows precisely the various courses of action available to them, God can formulate in advance an effective response to any course of action they may choose.

The other basis for affirming God's ultimate sovereignty is His infinite superiority to the creatures. As their Creator, God knows the range of options available to His creatures. He also is Himself responsible for those options. God determined how much freedom to allow His creatures. In so doing He limited the extent of their potential disruption of the universe. Surely God retains sufficient power to ensure the ultimate realization of His objectives. Foreseeing every possible development and possessing infinite wisdom and power, God can formulate and implement a course of action perfectly appropriate to every situation. God thus has certain objectives for His creation. He also has alternative ways of achieving these objectives. Which course of action He selects depends upon the choices of His creatures. So they do indeed contribute to the actual course of history. But the ultimate end of history is in God's hands.

William James used the analogy of two chess players to show how divine providence and human freedom are compatible.[1] If one player is an international grand master and the other a mere novice, the outcome of the game never remains in doubt. The grand master can conclude it with a few decisive moves any time he chooses. He can do so not because he knows in advance everything that will happen. Neither does he plan every move the novice will make. The beginner is free to do whatever he chooses. But the master knows exactly how to respond to anything he tries. Because of the master's superior skill, there is no possible development for which he will be unprepared. Thus the eventual outcome of the game is a foregone conclusion. But the precise course of action leading up to it will reflect the decisions of both players.

Similarly, the final outcome of history is a practical certainty. God's objectives for mankind will eventually be realized, what-

---

[1]William James, *The Will to Believe and Other Essays* (London: Longmans, Green & Co., 1897), pp. 181, 182, cited in John Hick, *Evil and the God of Love*, p. 344.

ever the actual course of events may be. Because God's resources are infinitely superior to those of His creatures, He can respond to all their decisions with complete adequacy. This does not mean that He either knows or plans in advance everything that happens. God maintains ultimate sovereignty over history. But He does not exercise absolute control.

History will ultimately fulfill God's objectives for humanity. But this does not mean that His will is realized in the case of every human being. On the individual level God's designs are often thwarted. The Bible says that God desires the salvation of all men (1 Tim. 2:4; 2 Pet. 3:9). But not all men accept salvation. Many will eventually be lost (see Matt. 25:41; Rev. 19:12–15). Consequently, while a person may not prevent the realization of God's overall purposes, he may certainly interfere with God's intentions for his own life.

This is clear from the experiences of a number of prominent people in the Bible. It is apparent that God had a specific role for certain individuals to play in life. This was true of figures such as Moses (Ex. 3:7–10), Samson (Judges 13:2–5), Saul (1 Sam. 9:15–17), David (1 Sam. 16:1, 11–13), Jeremiah (Jer. 1:4–5), Ezekiel (Ezek. 2:3–5), and John the Baptist (Luke 1:13–17). But it does not follow that God's plans for every human being are just as specific. Persons who received a divine call to a particular work were the exception in the Bible, rather than the rule. Nor does it follow that even these individuals had no choice but to accept God's plan for their lives. For example, God warned Ezekiel of the dire consequences of neglecting his responsibilities as a prophet, which indicates that he could have done so (Ezek. 3:16–21). Saul failed to fulfill God's plan for his life (1 Sam. 15:11) as did a number of Israel's kings. And there were incidents in the lives of some of the others just mentioned that were not in harmony with God's will (see Num. 20:7–12; 2 Sam. 11). So a divine call does not guarantee the fulfillment of God's purposes in a person's life.

We have seen that God's providential power involves a creative response to events as they happen. It also ensures the ultimate fulfillment of His broad purposes for human beings. Another aspect of God's infinite resourcefulness is His capacity to work for good in every situation, however negative it may appear.

Imagine a sculptor at work on a block of marble. Suppose his original plans are interrupted when his chisel uncovers a streak of discoloration running through the block. A lesser artist would abandon the effort. But he continues, carefully modifying his plans for the piece as he works. When he is finished, the inherent flaw in the material is perfectly incorporated within the design. Instead of detracting from the beauty of the overall composition, it actually enhances it. This capacity to modify one's intention in the middle of things calls for a higher kind of creative genius than that which knows of the flaw in advance and makes allowances for it from the beginning.

God also responds to developments within the temporal world as they occur, even when they are inherently at odds with His purposes. He so incorporates them within His plans that they actually contribute to the fulfillment of His ultimate purposes. Such a picture presents us with a more exalted view of divine providence than the more conventional one.

The notion that God can incorporate anything into His plan and work through it for good also has enormous practical religious value. Paul said, "We know that in everything God works for good with those who love him, who are called according to his purpose" (Rom. 8:28). We sometimes take these words to indicate that everything which happens to someone is part of an inflexible divine plan for his life. But this makes God directly responsible for all that happens. Indeed, it assigns inherent positive value to every experience. Nothing is contrary to the will of God. Personal tragedies and disappointments, suffering and illness, are all part of God's inscrutable will for our lives. Someday we will see all that has happened from the perspective of eternity. Then we will discover that everything was for the best.

The fundamental problem with this view is not its affirmation that the course of our lives ultimately conforms to a design for which God is responsible. The problem is that it attributes every experience to God's specific intention. And this puts God in the position of intending some individuals to commit certain sins. According to this model, for example, God probably intended the thief on the cross to commit his crimes in order to obtain salvation at the side of Jesus before his death.

By contrast the open view of God can relieve Him of responsibility for such things. It maintains instead that God did not intend many of the things which happen to us. But once they occur, God nevertheless responds to them in a way that somehow benefits us. Thus, if one is open to divine leading, something as tragic as the death of a parent in one's childhood, though not intended by God, can nevertheless result in certain benefits not otherwise likely to occur.

In other words, something that happens in spite of God's will can make a positive contribution to one's life, because God can bring beneficial results out of it. This means that anything—no matter how negative in itself—can become the occasion for good as a result of God's infinite resourcefulness. With this in mind, an individual can look back on his life, take it all into account—the bad and the good alike—and tell himself that nothing is totally wasted. God can incorporate everything into His ultimate design.

One of Arthur Maxwell's children's stories illustrates this point. A frail girl found her only pleasure in playing a simple piece on the piano in the lobby of a hotel her father managed. Her repetition of the tedious tune predictably irritated the hotel guests. One day they were about to stop her when they suddenly heard beautiful music coming from the piano. As they looked into the lobby they saw the little girl still pounding out her simple tune. But beside her sat a professional musician. He was watching her hands carefully and accompanying her notes with magnificent chords and arpeggios. Their combined efforts produced a skilled performance.

We can think of God as a composer of infinite skill and of ourselves as producing the most rudimentary form of music. But He responds to our halting efforts and incorporates each of them, even the mistakes, into a symphony of transcendent grandeur. So great is His creative genius that nothing we do is cast aside. Every note, however apparently discordant, receives a fitting place in the final work.

The claim that nothing can thwart the fulfillment of God's

objectives for our lives needs another qualification, which Paul's famous statement provides. As we have seen, it is not the case that all things work together for good of their own accord, as if all things were essentially good. It is God who works in them for good. Without His creative response to the disappointments and tragedies of life, little good—if any—would result. We also need to keep in mind the closing words of Paul's statement in Romans 8:28: "with those who love him, who are called according to his purpose." Paul does not mean that God helps only His favorites, that He works for good only in the lives of a privileged few. God is always at work for good. He seeks to make the best of things in every human life. But the fact remains that He can do more for those who respond to His creative power than for those who resist it.

The extent to which God can work for good in a person's life largely depends on his willingness to learn from God's instruction. People from the same family may respond to the same tragedy in quite different ways. Whether they grow bitter or stronger depends on their response to God's attempts to work for good. There is a limit, then, to God's ability to overrule evil for good. Not on the cosmic scale, where His overall purposes will be realized no matter what happens along the way. But on the individual level, where His infinite capacity to work for good requires our willingness to trust Him. In the lives of those who love Him God does indeed work for good in everything. Nothing can remove them from His love and care. He can use everything that happens to them for their ultimate benefit.

We have argued that God's infinite resourcefulness mitigates the consequences of evil in our lives. Therefore nothing, however opposed to His will, lies beyond God's capacity to work for good. This may create the impression that in the final analysis everything essentially conforms to God's plan and nothing is ultimately evil.

The impression that evil is less than entirely negative also draws support from the fact that certain values would never have existed in the absence of evil. On the human side, courage requires the reality of danger; penitence, the existence of sin; compassion, the presence of suffering; and forgiveness, the experience of mistreatment. And on the divine side, God's grace is often thought to presuppose the occurrence of human sin, which provided God an opportunity to manifest this particular quality of character. Hence, the *felix culpa* theme in the ancient Easter liturgy. It describes Adam's fall as the necessary and fortunate occasion for Christ's redemptive death.

Now, it is true that certain values presuppose the presence of evil. But the emergence of these values does not transform the evil into something inherently good. A widow with young children to raise may learn self-reliance and efficiency to a degree impossible had her husband lived. But this will hardly lead her to give thanks for his death. So it is one thing to say that nothing, however negative, lies beyond God's capacity to work for good. But it is quite another to say that nothing is essentially negative. In order to avoid leaving the impression that God's infinite resourcefulness somehow eliminates all evil, we need to emphasize two additional points.

One is the fact that whatever benefits may follow some evil thing or some tragic experience, they are due entirely to God's response to it and to His ability to evoke certain attitudes on the part of human beings. The benefits do not indicate the presence of positive qualities or redeeming features in the experience itself. The injuries sustained by the victims of a horrible traffic accident may put the members of an emergency-room staff to the supreme test of their skill. Their effectiveness may reach new heights in response to the challenge. They may even perform better in subsequent situations. But this does not make the accident itself a fortunate event. So, we must not regard the evil that occasions something good as anything less than evil in itself. God's resourcefulness does not transform evil into something good.

Another consideration prevents us from regarding as less than wholly evil the evil that occasions something good. Evil always results in a situation that is worse than what otherwise *could* have been the case. This is true even when some of the beneficial consequences of evil would be absent. A home without a father is less than ideal, no matter how admirably the mother manages on her own. By God's grace, benefits may follow the occurrence of evil. However, the net effect of evil is still negative. It always involves a loss.

The sculptor of our earlier illustration modified his design to accommodate the discoloration in the marble. And the effect may have displayed certain aspects of his skill more dramatically than would the original design. But the final sculpture may well have been less beautiful than what he could have produced with flawless material. Similarly, the reality of sin occasions a display of God's love and resourcefulness that would not have been possible in an unfallen universe. But this does not mean that the world as a whole is better off as a result of sin. The overall results, the net effects, are ultimately negative, for evil involves an irrecoverable loss. History does not lose its tragic character by reason of divine providence.

Evil remains essentially evil in spite of God's creative response to it. Sin's net effects are always negative. Such a recognition should prevent Christians from a distorted reaction to unpleasant experiences. Some people try to maintain an uninterrupted awareness of God's care for their lives by making it a habit to credit God with everything that happens to them. Mistreatment, physical handicaps, financial setbacks—they attribute them all to God's inscrutable design for their lives.

A popular lecturer in conservative Christian circles encourages young people to regard every parental decision as the manifest will of God for their lives, even when the parents make no profession of religion. The motive behind this advice is commendable. However, it leads to the potentially harmful conclusion that God's intentions lie behind everything that happens to us. The effect of such thinking makes God the author of evil. We should think of the good that God accomplishes as happening in spite of evil, not because of it. We may "in every thing give thanks" (1 Thess. 5:18, KJV), as the apostle enjoins, but we should do so because God never forsakes us, not because He plans everything that happens to us.

The open view of God thus suggests a concept of providence that exhibits the following features: First, since God relates to the creaturely world in dynamic interaction, providence involves God's creative response to events as they happen. It is not the outworking of an invariant primordial plan, fixed from the ages of eternity.

Second, this understanding of providence distinguishes between ultimate sovereignty and absolute control. On the grand scale, God directs the course of history. However, He is not responsible for everything that actually happens. Other agents make their contribution too. He will achieve His ultimate objectives for human life but not His will for every human being. On the individual level God's designs are often thwarted.

Finally, this view of providence affirms both the infinite resourcefulness of God and the essential ineradicable negative nature of evil. God can work for good no matter how desperate the situation. But the net effect of evil is exactly that—evil. No matter how much good results, evil is never "more than made up for." It involves permanent loss.

With this concept of providence we can affirm the ultimate triumph of God's love. At the same time we can maintain our instinctive reaction to evil as something that ought not to be and that God does not desire.

7

**Prophecy and the
Openness of God**

However the open view of God enriches the doctrine of providence, many Christians will question its acceptability in light of
other biblical ideas. Some of these concepts appear rather clearly
to support the traditional view of God's relation to the world.
Two biblical teachings that come readily to mind are prophecy
and predestination. These concepts seem to indicate, respectively, that God knows the entire future in advance and that He
controls its course in detail. In order to confirm the theological
validity of our open view of God, therefore, we need to explain
its relation to these two biblical ideas. This chapter deals with
prophecy. The next discusses foreknowledge and predestination.

Prophecy plays an important part in the biblical portrait of
God. Like the great works of creation (Isa. 45:12, 18) and salvation (Deut. 26:7–9; Isa. 45:8, 21–22; Tit. 2:11), it is one of the things
that distinguish God from everything else. "I am God and there
in none like me, declaring the end from the beginning and from
ancient times things not yet done" (Isa. 46:9, 10). In Chapter 6
we saw that the open view of God's experience leads to a more
complex and ultimately richer concept of divine providence than
the customary one. It also involves a similarly complicated view
of prophecy.

The conventional understanding of predictive prophecy is

that God peers into the future from His exalted vantage point and provides us with a preview of coming events. For if God exhaustively knows the future, He can simply tell us what He sees will happen, much as we can turn a few pages ahead in a book we are reading to see how the story turns out. Prophecy is possible, on this view, because the future is entirely predictable.

We have examined some of the major difficulties of this view of the future, such as its exclusion of human freedom and divine sensitivity. Equally significant is the fact that this view of prophecy fails to do justice to the biblical perspective.

The Hebrews and early Christians were not unique in believing in prophecy. Prophets and soothsayers were common figures in the ancient world. According to the Bible, even false prophets could occasionally predict the future accurately (see Deut. 13:1–3). What distinguishes the biblical view of prophecy from that of other peoples was the concept of time or history it involved.

For classical thinkers, time moves in great cycles. The future is the inevitable consequence of the past, and nothing really new ever happens. On this view, prophecy is the extrapolation of the future from the past, and it is neither remarkable nor particularly difficult. To the Greek historian Polybius, for example, it was an easy matter to foretell the future, because the future is already determined.[1] What will happen is the inevitable outcome of what has already happened.

In contrast to the cyclical view of time, the biblical writers espoused what is commonly described as a linear concept. They believed that history is going somewhere, rather than constantly repeating itself. The reason for this view was their concept of history as the arena of God's activity (e.g. Deut. 26:5–9; 7:1; Isa. 48:20–21; 61:1, 2; Luke 4:16–21; 2 Cor. 5:19–21). They believed that God is active in human affairs, achieving His purposes and working to bring history to a climax (2 Pet. 3:9–13). Consequently, for them the future is essentially unpredictable. We can't know what is going to happen, unless God chooses to reveal it to us (see Matt. 24:36).

---

[1]See Karl Löwith, *Meaning in History* (Chicago: University of Chicago Press, 1949), p. 9.

This view of time entails a distinctive view of prophecy. In contrast to other concepts, biblical prophecy is not sheer prognostication. Its primary purpose is not to express the inevitable outcome of the past, even though it may do this on occasion, as we shall see. Instead, its fundamental purpose is to reveal the will of a personal Being, declaring His intentions to accomplish certain things. So the biblical view of prophecy goes hand in hand with our open view of God. It emphasizes the openness of the future and the dynamic nature of God's relation to the world. This view of prophecy has two important consequences. It requires a careful interpretation of divine predictions, and it gives an integrity to conditional prophecies that the ordinary view lacks.

Let us begin by examining various ways of interpreting predictive prophecies. Our purpose in suggesting such models is not to provide formulas that will precisely fit every, or even any, specific prophecy. We only wish to show that the phenomenon of predictive prophecy is compatible with the concept of divine openness presented in this book. The following discussion therefore assumes that biblical prophecies intend to convey information about the future. The question is how they can do so if the future is genuinely open, and God does not possess absolute foreknowledge.

Divine predictions may express one thing or a combination of several different things. They may, to begin with, express God's knowledge of what will occur in the future as the inevitable consequence of factors already present (e.g. Jer. 37:6–10). Since God's knowledge of the present is exhaustive, his knowledge of the future must be unimaginably extensive. This provides a possible explanation of God's ability to account for events in the distant future, events that may seem highly improbable at present.

For example, a skilled physician can predict the death of a seemingly healthy individual because he perceives symptoms that escape the untrained eye. Likewise, God may describe apparently unlikely events in the relatively remote future because He knows and understands the present exhaustively. Possibly this explains prophecies concerning the demise of one nation and the ascendancy of another, like those found in Daniel 2. God must be able to chart the future course of history in significant detail if He knows everything about the present, even on the view that the future is to some extent open.

Divine predictions may also express God's own intentions to act in a certain way. Some of the things God predicts will happen because He intends to make them happen by taking direct action Himself. Some texts are thought to support absolute foreknowledge: "I am God, and there is none like me, declaring the end from the beginning and from ancient times things not yet done" (Isa. 46:9, 10). Yet we find texts in close proximity that relate God's predictions to His own activity: "I have spoken, and I will bring it to pass; I have purposed, and I will do it" (Isa. 46:11). "The former things I declared of old, they went forth from my mouth and I made them known; then suddenly I did them and they came to pass" (Isa. 48:3). So God announced certain things because He planned to do them Himself. Many Christians would see a clear expression of such divine intention in the biblical promises of Christ's return. They believe that the glorious parousia will result from the intervention of God in human history. It does not result from the natural outworking of events. Indeed, they believe that the Second Coming will eventually occur no matter what course human history takes in the meantime (Heb. 10:35–37).

Predictive prophecy may also represent a combination of the two factors just described. That is to say, a specific prophecy may express both God's knowledge of what will happen *and* His own intention to act in a certain way. This may provide an alternative to the traditional explanation of Isaiah 44:28—45:4, a classic example of predictive prophecy. According to conservative biblical scholarship, these verses designated Cyrus as the restorer of Israel's fortunes more than a century before his birth. For many people this prophecy indicates that God can simply look into the future, see what's going to happen, and make an announcement. In other words, this prophecy implies that the future must be there for God to see. But this is not the only explanation. God may have perceived factors that indicated the decline of Babylon and the rise of Persia a hundred years ahead. He also must have known the ancestors of Cyrus and foreseen the possibility of his birth. In addition, God may have been actively involved in bringing events to the place where this prophecy would be fulfilled.

Admittedly, there is no way to calculate the relation in a given prophecy between what God can foresee as the direct result of present factors and what will happen as the result of His personal activity. But we cannot exclude the possibility that both elements play a part in many biblical prophecies. So, even predictive prophecies pertaining to what appears to us to have been the very remote future do not necessarily require the traditional understanding of divine foreknowledge.

Therefore, some prophecies express God's knowledge of what will happen, His own intention to do specific things, or some combination of the two. In addition, other prophecies express God's intention to act in a certain way if a particular course of action obtains or if people behave a certain way. These are customarily referred to as "conditional prophecies." Their fulfillment depends—or is conditional—upon the way their recipients respond to them. Jeremiah 18:7–10 provides a clear description of conditional prophecy: "If at any time I declare concerning a nation or a kingdom, that I will pluck up and break down and destroy it, and if that nation, concerning which I have spoken, turns from its evil, I will repent of the evil that I intended to do to it. And if at any time I declare concerning a nation or a kingdom that I will build and plant it, and if it does evil in my sight, not listening to my voice, then I will repent of the good which I had intended to do to it."

The best known example of such a prophecy may be Jonah's announcement that Nineveh would be destroyed in forty days (Jon. 3:4). The destruction did not occur as predicted because the city's inhabitants repented in response to Jonah's message. And "when God saw what they did, how they turned from their evil way, God repented of the evil which he had said he would do to them; and he did not do it" (Jon. 3:10).

Jonah's experience suggests that the real purpose of conditional prophecy is not to provide information about the future. Conditional prophecy is intended to evoke a positive response to God in the present. Indeed, this is the only way to make sense out of it. For if God intended simply to destroy Nineveh, willy-nilly, there was no reason to send Jonah with his announcement. What would that have accomplished? If, however, God intended to destroy Nineveh only if its citizens failed to change their ways, then Jonah's mission becomes intelligible. God wanted to enable and encourage the Ninevites to avert their impending destruction.

This brings us to an interesting question. Did God know that the Ninevites would repent when He sent Jonah to preach? The classical view of foreknowledge requires that He did, of course. But if so, the announcement of impending destruction did not express something God really planned to do. If He knew for sure they would repent, He also knew He would not destroy the city. The announcement was made solely to produce the desired effect. If, on the other hand, their response to Jonah's message remained indefinite until they actually made it, we can assume that the threat expressed a genuine divine intention. In view of their wickedness, God planned to destroy the city. He was really going to do it. Jonah wasn't just saying so. Accordingly, God decided not to destroy Nineveh only when their repentance was evident.

If it is true that creaturely decisions are not foreknowable and that reality is open to some extent, then conditional prophecies acquire new integrity. They express genuine divine intentions. They represent invitations to actually change the course of events. At face value, conditional prophecies indicate a real interaction between God and the creaturely world. They imply that what men and women do is indefinite to a significant extent and therefore unknowable until these decisions are made. In contrast, the concept of absolute foreknowledge removes the "if" from (so-called) conditional prophecies. According to the customary view, the future is definite. God already knows exactly what He will do. Correspondingly, it reduces biblical descriptions of God as "repenting" or "changing His mind" to the status of anthropomorphisms. And this is just how many commentaries and systematic theologies interpret such expressions. As a result, they detract from the dramatic portrait of God's interaction with the world which the Bible provides.

We typically apply the category of conditional prophecy to predictions which were not fulfilled, such as Jonah's announcement of Nineveh's destruction. But it is important to recognize that many predictions that came to pass were also conditional. A good example is Jeremiah's prediction that Jerusalem would be destroyed by the invading Babylonians (Jer. 32:4). In time the city was devastated, just as Jeremiah predicted (Jer. 52:12–14), so it provides us with a clear case of fulfilled prophecy. But another of Jeremiah's prophecies indicates that the destruction of Jerusalem was contingent on the action of Zedekiah, the last king of Judah. If he surrendered to the princes of the king of Babylon, Jeremiah assured him, the city would be spared; if he didn't, Jerusalem would be destroyed (Jer. 38:17–18). As it turned out, Zedekiah refused to surrender, and the city suffered the consequences. Its destruction fulfilled a conditional prophecy.

It is possible that other fulfilled prophecies were also conditional. Perhaps this is true of the famous prophecy concerning Cyrus mentioned above. If Cyrus had refused to repatriate the Jews, we would no doubt interpret Isaiah's prediction as a conditional prophecy. So there is no compelling reason to deny that it was conditional even though it was fulfilled.

A salient feature of conditional prophecy needs to be applied to prophecy in general. Conditional prophecy summons people to a relationship with God. It vividly reminds them that the future depends on their response to Him. The primary purpose of all prophecy is to evoke a positive response to God. God seeks to establish a saving relationship with human beings in all His communications. Biblical prophecy is never presented merely as a source of information for the detached or disinterested observer. It always involves a call to decision. It is always an invitation to respond to God in the present.

At first glance, the phenomenon of prophecy seems to pose a problem for the open view of God. People often assume that it proves the validity of absolute foreknowledge. But careful investigation reveals something quite different. Properly understood, biblical prophecy gives strong support to the open view of God. It shows that the course of history is not a foregone conclusion. And it reveals that God's relation to the world is dynamic and dramatic.

8

Predestination and the Openness of God

For many people the most formidable problem for an open view of reality and of God will no doubt be the apparent discrepancy, or at least tension, between this view and certain biblical passages. Scripture specifically attributes to God the activities of "foreknowing" and "predestining." In a number of instances the Bible describes God as knowing the course of individual lives and specific personal decisions well in advance. This chapter will deal systematically with these different types of biblical statements. It will attempt to show that they can all be reconciled with the view that God's experience of the creaturely world is open rather than closed.

The Greek New Testament speaks of God as "foreknowing" three times (Rom. 8:29; 11:2; 1 Pet. 1:20), as having "foreknowledge" two times (Acts 2:23; 1 Pet. 1:2), and as "predestining" or "deciding beforehand" four times (Acts 4:28; Rom. 8:29; 1 Cor. 2:7; Eph. 1:5). In each instance, the word refers to some aspect of salvation history as the fulfillment of a preexistent plan. And the use of such expressions as "before the foundation of the world" (1 Pet. 1:20; Eph. 1:4) and "before the ages" (1 Cor. 2:7) indicates that the plan existed as early as Creation.

Jesus' death occured in harmony with this plan. Those who put Him to death were acting in harmony with it. "This Jesus, delivered up according to the definite plan and foreknowledge of God, you crucified and killed by the hands of lawless men" (Acts 2:23). "For truly in this city there were gathered together against thy holy servant Jesus, whom thou didst anoint, both Herod and Pontius Pilate, with the Gentiles and the peoples of Israel, to do whatever thy hand and thy plan had predestined to take place" (Acts 4:27, 28). "He [Christ] was destined before the foundation of the world but was made manifest at the end of the times for your sake" (1 Pet. 1:20).

God's saving activity also included the creation of certain human communities. The New Testament describes both the nation of Israel and the members of the Christian church as objects of divine foreknowledge and/or predestination. "For those whom he foreknew he also predestined to be conformed to the image of his Son, in order that he might be the first-born among many brethren. And those whom he predestined he also called; and those whom he called he also justified; and those whom he justified he also glorified" (Rom. 8:29, 30). "God has not rejected his people whom he foreknew" (Rom. 11:2). "He chose us in him before the foundation of the world, that we should be holy and blameless before him. He destined us in love to be his sons through Jesus Christ, according to the purpose of his will" (Eph. 1:4, 5). "To the exiles of the Dispersion in Pontus, Galatia, Capadocia, Asia, and Bithynia, chosen and destined by God the Father and sanctified by the Spirit for obedience to Jesus Christ and for sprinkling with his blood" (1 Pet. 1:1, 2).

Many people think that these biblical statements straightforwardly support the traditional view of God's relation to the temporal world. In their opinion God definitely knew when He created man that sin would arise and that the plan of salvation would be needed; it was impossible for Christ to sin; God knew in advance the identity of all who would ever accept salvation; and the enemies of God fulfilled His specific will for their individual lives. Contrary to the conventional interpretation, however, these and similar biblical statements do not require these conclusions. They can also be interpreted in harmony with the open view of God.

To begin with, the existence of a plan for human salvation as early as Creation does not necessarily indicate God definitely knew that man would sin before He created him. It may indicate only that God was aware that sin was a distinct possibility with man's creation, rather than a future actuality, and that He was fully prepared to meet the situation should it arise.

It is evident from the statements quoted that the mission of Jesus Christ was central to God's plan. His victory over sin was essential to man's salvation. But this does not mean that His success was a foregone conclusion, guaranteed from all eternity. Several biblical passages indicate quite the opposite.

For example, the Gospel's accounts of Jesus' temptations in the wilderness depict a genuine struggle on His part (Matt. 4:1–11; Mark 1:12, 13; Luke 4:1–13). Indeed, the constancy of His trust and obedience to God was so severely tested that He required the ministry of angels for physical survival (Matt. 4:11; compare Mark 1:13).

Similarly, the descriptions of Jesus' experience in Gethsemane the night of His betrayal reflect the conviction that His ultimate commitment to His Father's will was fully decided only then and there. It was not something settled from the outset of His life (Luke 22:42).

According to the author of the Epistle to the Hebrews, Jesus' temptations qualify Him, in part, to serve as our high priest: "For we have not a high priest who is unable to sympathize with our weaknesses, but one who in every respect has been tempted as we are, yet without sin" (4:15; compare 2:18). And he, too, emphasizes their genuineness, recalling the Gethsemane experience: "In the days of his flesh, Jesus offered up prayers and supplications, with loud cries and tears, to him who was able to save him from death, and he was heard for his godly fear" (Heb. 5:7).

When the New Testament refers to the temptations of Jesus, therefore, it presents them as genuine tests of His commitment to God. His victory was not the inevitable outworking of a predetermined and invariant pattern. The Bible thus supports the view that the success of Christ's mission was achieved during the actual course of His earthly life. It could not have been a foregone conclusion. For if He merely recited a well-rehearsed script, His moral experience could not have been genuine and

His victory would have been hollow.

Some biblical statements indicate that Christ's enemies and executioners in the final analysis acted in harmony with God's plan (Acts 2:23; 4:28). But this need not mean that their actions were predetermined and that they were simply doing what God planned and/or foresaw for them. Two considerations prevent this conclusion.

First, the Bible holds them accountable for their actions. The New Testament writers recoil from the specter of Christ's mistreatment. They view the perpetrators of these acts as responsible for their conduct. Acts, for examples, describes them as "lawless men" (2:23).

Second, the idea that anyone who pursues a path to perdition is doing what God wants him to do contradicts an essential theme in the New Testament. God desires the salvation of all men (1 Tim. 2:4; cf. Tit. 2:11). He has no pleasure in the death of the wicked (Ezek. 33:11), and is unwilling that any should perish (2 Pet. 3:9). If the criminal behavior of certain people is essential to God's plan for them, He hardly appears desirous of all men's salvation.

The great proponents of divine determinism frankly concede this point. For John Calvin and Jonathan Edwards, God does not will the salvation of all men: He predestines some to eternal life and others to eternal damnation.[1] Indeed, for them God wills everything that comes to pass, good and bad alike.[2] At the same time, they insist that God is not directly responsible for sin. Of the wicked Calvin states, "Their perdition depends upon the predestination of God in such way that the cause and occasion of it are found in themselves."[3] And according to Edwards, "There is no inconsistency in supposing, that God may hate a thing as it is in itself, and considered simply as evil, and yet that it may be his will it should come to pass, considering all consequences."[4] To summarize their position, God's overall plan re-

---

[1]*Institutes of the Christian Religion*, III.xxi.5, trans. Ford Lewis Battles (Philadelphia: Westminster Press, 1960), p. 926.

[2]*Institutes*, III.xxiii.8, p. 956.

[3]*Ibid.*, p. 957.

[4]*Freedom of the Will*, ed. Paul Ramsey (New Haven and London: Yale University Press, 1957), p. 407.

quires the existence of evil, and He orders things in such a way that sin is inevitable, but He is not directly responsible for it. Strictly speaking, He causes sin to happen, but He does not cause the sin itself.

The arguments are ingenious but unconvincing. Scripture and logic alike require us to view sin as fundamentally and permanently opposed to God's will (see James 1:13; 1 John 1:5). If sin and damnation were part of his original design for human history, then He bears responsibility for their occurrence, however we describe the immediate agency involved. As a basic principle of Christian faith, we can never attribute sin or its consequences to the will of God.

For these reasons we must look for another interpretation of the biblical statements that those who sinned fulfilled God's plan. Our open view of reality and divine providence suggests the following: God's opponents do not do what He wants them to. But He can respond to their actions in a way that serves His purposes. Consequently, it is not the evil act itself that fulfills God's purposes, it is God's response to it, or the use He makes of the act, that works for good. Furthermore, God can so modify the implementation of His plan to developing circumstances that any decision somehow contributes, even though it may be inherently opposed to His will.

The New Testament most frequently refers to members of the Christian church as objects of divine foreknowledge and predestination (Rom. 8:29; Eph. 1:5; 1 Pet. 1:2). And in one place *foreknow* is applied to the people of Israel (Rom. 11:2). From these instances, some conclude that God knows in advance, even from all eternity, exactly who will eventually be saved. We have already seen that such a notion excludes genuine freedom. But it also misses the essential point of these particular statements. The biblical references to people as objects of God's foreknowledge or predestination are typically concerned with corporate election. They do not refer to personal salvation.

The outstanding instance of divine election is God's choice of Israel as His special people. This choice provides the background for the New Testament concepts of foreknowledge and predestination. The nature and purpose of Israel's election have attracted extensive scholarly attention, and we can do little more than delineate its major features here.

To begin with, God's election of Israel was fundamentally a gracious invitation. It was not an announcement of fate. Neither was it inevitable destiny. It was not as if the Israelites had no choice in the matter. God was not informing them of what had to be the case. Instead, He was telling them what could be the case if they cooperated. This does not mean that God presented the invitation as a take-it-or-leave-it matter. He never acted as if their response were of little importance. To the contrary, their response either way entailed serious consequences. But they could choose to refuse their election as God's special people. God's call represented an opportunity, not a necessity.

The calls to obedience throughout Hebrew Scripture reflect the conditional nature of Israel's election. Along with assurances of God's gracious love, one finds warnings of divine wrath and discipline. "Know therefore that the Lord your God is God, the faithful God who keeps covenant and steadfast love with those who love him and keep his commandments, to a thousand generations, and requites to their face those who hate him, by destroying them; he will not be slack with him who hates him, he will requite him to his face. You shall therefore be careful to do the commandment, and the statutes, and the ordinances, which I command you this day" (Deut. 7:9–11).

A second feature of Israel's election was its basis in divine grace. God did not choose the Israelites in response to any attractive features they exhibited. The Israelites had nothing to recommend them to God. God did not choose them because they were larger than other nations: "It was not because you were more in number than any other people that the Lord set his love upon you and chose you, for you were the fewest of all peoples" (Deut. 7:7). Nor did He select them because of some superior righteousness: "Not because of your righteousness or the uprightness of your heart are you going in to possess their land" (Deut. 9:5). God's choice lay solely in His love: "It is because the Lord loves you, and is keeping the oath which he swore to your fathers, that the Lord has brought you out with a mighty hand, and redeemed you from the house of bondage, from the hand of Pharaoh king of Egypt" (Deut. 7:8). As far as nations go, then, the Israelites were weak and insignificant. God's call was solely a matter of grace. It rested entirely on God's initiative. It provided no basis for self-congratulation.

The Scriptures repeatedly emphasize the fact that Israel owed its very existence to God's grace. One example is the biblical account of Isaac's birth to Abraham and Sarah long after she had passed her childbearing years (Gen. 18:10, 11; 21:1–7). Contrary as it was to the natural course of events, Isaac's birth demonstrated that the fulfillment of the promise to make of Abraham a great nation depended on divine power, not on human resources.

Paul emphasized the wholly gracious character of Israel's election. He pointed to God's preference of Jacob over Esau, the twin sons of Isaac and Rebekah. God expressed His preference before their birth, "though they were not yet born and had done nothing either good or bad" (Rom. 9:11). To Paul this demonstrated that election is based solely on God's will. It is in no sense a response to human qualifications. "So it depends not upon man's will or exertion, but upon God's mercy" (verse 16).

A third feature of Israel's election is that it involved a summons to service, not an elevation to privilege. The Israelites were not simply called. God called them to do something. Specifically, they were supposed to extend the knowledge of God to other nations and ultimately to the whole world. By precept and example, the Israelites were to enlighten the earth with an understanding of God's saving power. As a later prophet lyrically described it, "I will give you as a light to the nations, that my salvation may reach to the end of the earth" (Isa. 49:6; compare 42:6). God's call thus provided no basis for feelings of exclusivism and superiority. It did set Israel apart, but only for the purpose of rendering service to others.

The call of the Israelites also illustrates the fundamentally corporate nature of divine election. By and large, God's call pertains to a group, or a people, rather than to an individual. And when an individual is specifically mentioned, it is usually in view of the group that the individual represents. When a prophet invoked the name *Jacob*, for example, typically he had in mind the whole people of Israel (e.g. Num. 24:17).

This interrelation of individual and group is sometimes expressed as the concept of "corporate personality." According to the classic study of this concept, "the whole group, including its past, present and future members, might function as a single individual through any one of those members conceived as representative of it."[5]

What does this mean? The Bible may speak of an individual as the recipient of God's call, when in fact it is the group of which the individual is a part and whom the individual represents that constitutes the ultimate object of election. In calling Abraham (Gen. 12:1–3; 15:5), for example, and in preferring Jacob to Esau, God was in effect calling their descendants, the Israelites. God's call had to do not with their individual destinies but with that of the people whom they represented.

To summarize, the primary object of divine election is the group, not the individual. In addition, divine election involves an invitation to service. It does not guarantee salvation. Its outcome is conditional upon the response of the people. It is not inevitable. And it has its basis solely in God's initiative, not in the recognition of deserving qualities in the object of election.

Many New Testament descriptions of the Christian church recall the essential features of Israel's election. To begin with, membership in the church is a matter of choice, not of fate. God compels no one to belong to the church. Furthermore, the danger of falling away is real, as admonitions like the following reveal: "Therefore, brethren, be the more zealous to confirm your call and election, for if you do this you will never fall" (2 Pet. 1:10). "Therefore let any one who thinks that he stands take heed lest he fall" (1 Cor. 10:12).

In the second place, the church owes its existence to divine grace and not to the qualities of its members. Indeed, its members are characteristically unimpressive on a human scale. Paul reminded the Corinthian believers of this: "Consider your call,

---

[5]H. Wheeler Robinson, "The Hebrew Conception of Corporate Personality," quoted in Edmond Jacob's *Theology of the Old Testament*, translated by Arthur W. Heathcote and Philip J. Allcock (New York: Harper & Row, Publishers, 1958), p. 154.

brethren; not many of you were wise according to worldly stan-
dards, not many were powerful, not many were of noble birth;
but God chose what is foolish in the world to shame the wise,
God chose what is weak in the world to shame the strong, God
chose what is low and despised in the world, even things that
are not, to bring to nothing things that are, so that no human
being might boast in the presence of God. He is the source of
your life in Christ Jesus" (1 Cor. 1:26–30).

Then, too, the church like Israel exists for service. It fulfills
its purpose by sharing with the world the news of God's gracious
action in Jesus Christ, as the Gospel Commission indicates (Matt.
28:19, 20).

And, finally, the concept of corporate personality plays an
important part in the New Testament understanding of the
church. So intimately are Christ and the church related that it is
described as His body. Paul frequently uses this metaphor. And
God elects Christians by virtue of their connection to Jesus, the
principle object of divine election. "He chose us in him before
the foundation of the world" (Eph. 1:4). Thus the church as a
corporate entity rather than a collection of individual believers
best expresses the New Testament concept.

In light of all this we see that the New Testament concepts of
foreknowledge and predestination have to do with the nature
and purpose of the church as a whole, especially in its relation
to Christ. These terms do not imply that God knew from eternity
the personal identity of all who will eventually be saved. For
when in the New Testament we read "predestination" and "foreknowledge," the author has in mind the group. Individuals can
fail and fall away, as the frequent admonitions and exhortations
to watchfulness indicate. But the destiny of the church as a whole
is assured.

We can illustrate this distinction between the group and the
individual in the following way. At fall registration a college band
director may use glowing descriptions of the year's musical
schedule to encourage students to audition. He may say, "The
band will play at the White House at Thanksgiving, march in
the Rose Parade on New Year's Day, and travel to Hawaii in
April." He knows what the band as a whole will do. But he does

not know the individual identity of all its future members. Many students will never audition. Some will audition and fail. Others may pass and join the band, only to withdraw from school later. And some may join the band in midterm. The schedule of the band is one thing. The precise composition of the band is another.

Similarly, a group of people will eventually be saved. This group will ultimately fulfill God's hopes for humanity. The destiny of the group as a whole is predetermined. Its triumph is assured. But the precise composition of the group awaits the personal decisions of individual human beings. The salvation of the individual depends upon his positive response to God. In this way the biblical notions of predestination and foreknowledge are totally compatible with the concepts of personal freedom and an open reality.

Our discussion of the biblical notion of election helps explain certain biblical passages in which God seemed to know in advance the action of individuals. Some interpret God's words to Rebekah before the birth of her twin sons as evidence of absolute foreknowledge: "Two nations are in your womb, and two peoples, born of you, shall be divided; the one shall be stronger than the other, the elder shall serve the younger" (Gen. 25:23). But God's preference of Jacob to Esau, as we have noticed, was an instance of divine election. As interpreted by Paul (Rom. 9:10–13), the words demonstrate that the call to Jacob was utterly independent of his future behavior. The eventual differences between the boys did not account for God's choice. In Paul's view that would contradict the gracious character of election. Rather, it was God's choice—and that alone—which accounted for the different destinies of their descendants. So the statement does not express God's foreknowledge of the two son's characters. The corporate nature of election suggests that the essential point of the story has to do with the superiority of the Israelites to the Edomites, who were respectively represented by Jacob and Esau. The passage does not refer to the personal behavior of these two ancestral figures.

Not all the passages apparently describing God's knowledge of a person's future can be explained in terms of corporate personality, of course. In others an individual rather than a group is clearly intended. In some instances, God calls an individual to a specific work, such as that of a prophet. Jeremiah, for example, reported receiving the following message from the Lord: "Before I formed you in the womb I knew you, and before you were born I consecrated you: I appointed you a prophet to the nations" (Jer. 1:5).

Although Jeremiah's call involved an individual and not a group, it exhibits several of the features of election mentioned above. God called him to service rather than to a position of privilege. And it rested on divine initiative rather than human qualifications. Like other recipients of divine calls, such as Moses (Ex. 4:10), Jeremiah sought to excuse himself from the work (1:6). He felt inexperienced. But God assured him of divine support (verses 8, 19).

Moreover, nothing in the biblical narrative contradicts the idea that Jeremiah could have rejected the call. The call was an invitation to service or a command that he could disobey. But it was not an announcement of ineluctable fate. God may have called Jeremiah to the prophetic task contrary to his preferences, but He did not force him against his will. Consequently Jeremiah's experience does not support the idea that God foreknows the future absolutely and can ascertain every person's ultimate destiny. Prophetic calls are better understood as expressions of divine intention than as indications of absolute foreknowledge.

The Bible also indicates that God knew in advance the negative behavior of certain individuals. A familiar example is Pharaoh's refusal to free the Israelites at Moses' request. The writer of Exodus indicated that God informed Moses of Pharaoh's response well in advance. He variously attributed the hardness of Pharaoh's heart to the Lord—"I will harden . . . [Pharaoh's] heart" (4:21)—and to the monarch himself—"Pharaoh hardened his heart" (8:32). Indeed, in one place he stated of Pharaoh, "he sinned yet again, and hardened his heart" (9:34). These contrasting assignments of responsibility rule out an either-or answer to the question of who hardened Pharaoh's heart. And theological considerations as well prevent us from attributing it without qualification to God. We would hardly want to say that God made a person sin. So we must begin by attributing Pharaoh's hardness directly to himself. The king was himself responsible for refusing to obey the divine command. The task thus becomes one of interpreting the statements that God hardened the king's heart and of explaining how God knew this action in advance.

A possible interpretation of the statements that God hardened Pharaoh's heart is suggested by our earlier analysis of God's relation to the future. We noticed that perfect anticipation and absolute foreknowledge may appear quite similar in retrospect. However, their respective implications for God's relation to time are quite different. In light of Israel's dramatic deliverance from bondage, it is evident that God used the king's recalcitrance in a way that served His purposes: "For this purpose have I let you live, to show you my power, so that my name may be declared throughout all the earth" (Ex. 9:16). To someone looking at the king's behavior after the Exodus, it may have appeared that God intended the king's refusal all along, so perfectly did it serve His purposes. But such an interpretation seems to contradict the straightforward testimony of the biblical narrative. Let us consider an alternative.

The king's refusal may have been determined by his previous course of action. In view of Pharaoh's persistent oppression of the Hebrews, his response to the request for their release is not at all surprising. Indeed, it may have been entirely predictable to someone thoroughly familiar with his character. Knowing precisely the nature of Pharaoh's personality, God may have known that such a command would elicit only one response. Pharaoh's hardness of heart was, therefore, definite in advance. It was foreknowable to God because his previous behavior made certain his response to this particular situation. Thus, "God hardened his heart" only in the sense that He created a situation in which the monarch's behavior was determined completely by his character. Therefore it was entirely foreknowable.

Then, again, it is possible that the statements that God hardened Pharaoh's heart express His knowledge of what Pharaoh would in all probability do in response to Moses' request. They may not state what he could not help but do. That is to say, the king's response may have remained indefinite until he actually received the request, even though there was little likelihood that he would grant it. In any event, we are not left with the view either that God made the king refuse—he might have been genuinely free to grant the request—or that his refusal was from all eternity a foregone conclusion.

Similar considerations apply to other cases in the Bible where the misbehavior of certain individuals is foretold. Two well-known instances are Judas' betrayal and Peter's denial of Jesus. All four Gospels record Judas' action (Matt. 26:47–50; Mark 14:43–45; Luke 22:47, 48; John 18:2–5), and according to each account Jesus predicted it at the Last Supper (Matt. 26:20–25; Mark 14:18–21; Luke 22:21–23; John 13:18). Similarly, all four Gospels record Peter's threefold denial of Jesus (Matt. 26:69–74; Mark 14:66–72; Luke 22:54–62; John 18:17–27), as well as the fact that Jesus accurately foretold it (Matt. 26:34; Mark 14:30; Luke 22:34; John 13:38). The examples of Judas and Peter stand out in our minds, but Jesus also announced that all his disciples would forsake Him, citing the words of Zechariah 13:7, "Strike the shepherd, that the sheep may be scattered (Matt. 26:31; Mark 14:27). And, of course, the prediction was fulfilled (Matt. 26:51; Mark 14:50).

One interpretation of these statements is that Jesus' disciples could not avoid their actions. They simply played the role which fate assigned them. As we have seen, however, this view creates enormous problems. We shall explore other ways to interpret these statements.

One possibility is that Jesus foretold His disciples' behavior in order to warn them of the spiritual danger they were in. Sometimes a teacher will tell a student, "You're going to fail this semester," not to announce his final grade in the course, but to awaken him to his academic predicament and help him avert disaster while there is still time. Similarly, Jesus may have described Judas' plans in order to encourage him to abandon them. Perhaps He predicted the cowardice of Peter and the other disciples in hopes that they would take the necessary measures to correct their vulnerability. Some of Jesus' other statements that evening seem to support this view. He told Peter, for example, that He had prayed that his faith would not fail (Luke 23:32), and as He entered Gethsemane He urged the disciples, "Pray that you may not enter into temptation" (Luke 22:40).

Another possibility is that the behavior of Jesus' disciples that night was inevitable by the time of the Last Supper. Perhaps by then Judas had so committed himself to his course of action that there was no turning back, and the other disciples were so weak that it was impossible for them to give Jesus their support. With His astute insight into human behavior, or with divine aid, Jesus could have detected Judas' plans and perceived His disciples' weakness. On this view, Judas was free at an earlier time to avoid betraying Jesus, but his decision eventually became irreversible. Likewise, there was a time when the disciples might have prepared themselves for trial and danger, but they failed to do so, and now it was too late.

Although all the disciples abandoned Jesus the night of His arrest, the New Testament treats Judas' behavior as a special case. In the fourth Gospel, Jesus says of His betrayal, "it is that the scripture may be fulfilled," and quotes Psalm 41:9: "He who ate my bread has lifted his heel against me" (John 13:18). In the other Gospels Jesus says of the incident, "The Son of man goes as it is written of him" (Matt. 26:24) or words to that effect. And according to Acts, Peter said, "Brethren, the scripture had to be fulfilled which the Holy Spirit spoke beforehand by the mouth of David, concerning Judas who was guide to those who arrested Jesus" (Acts 1:16).

There is also evidence that Jesus referred to Judas' betrayal earlier in His ministry. According to John 6:70-71, "Jesus answered them, 'Did I not choose you, the twelve, and one of you is a devil?' He spoke of Judas the son of Simon Iscariot, for he, one of the twelve, was to betray him." To many, of course, such passages indicate that Judas' betrayal was a foregone conclusion long before—indeed centuries before—it occurred, and Judas had no alternative but to betray the Lord. But here again, there are other factors to consider.

One is the possibility that the prophecy applied to Judas was conditional. Granted, it was eventually fulfilled. But as we saw in the previous chapter, conditionality may apply to fulfilled prophecies as well as prophecies that were not fulfilled.

Another factor is the familiar tendency to look at a person's entire life in light of the single most dramatic or memorable thing that happened, especially if it occurs at the end. For example, it would be impossible for many people to think of Lee Harvey Oswald apart from the assassination of John F. Kennedy. No matter what part of his life they may consider, from early childhood to the day before the parade in Dallas, for them Oswald will always be the man who shot the President. The Gospel references to Judas seem to reflect this tendency. When he is listed with the disciples, his name always appears last, along with a reference to his future treachery (Matt. 10:4; Mark 3:19; Luke 6:16). For the other disciples, Judas was always "the one who would betray Jesus," from the very beginning of His ministry. This was the single most impressive thing about the man, and it colored every recollection of him.

A further consideration prevents us from concluding that Judas' action was unavoidable. This is the possibility that some of the prophecies fulfilled during the course of Jesus' life represent something other than a detailed and indelible forecast of the future. Perhaps such prophecies as Psalms 22:16–18 and 41:9 provided a general pattern of what might happen to Jesus, or a pattern that could apply to His life in more than one way. The fulfillment of these prophecies would still support the distinctive Christian claims for Jesus, but we would not be forced to conclude that the actions of many people during His life could not have been avoided. On this view, Judas' behavior indeed fulfilled the prophecy in question, but it may not have been the only possible way of fulfilling it. For example, Psalm 41:9 seems to apply to Peter's denial just as effectively as Judas' betrayal. With an approach like this, we can affirm both the validity of prophetic predictions and the integrity of human freedom.

We have examined a few of the best-known instances where the Bible describes prior knowledge of a person's behavior. It appears that none of them necessitates the classical notion of foreknowledge and/or predestination. When carefully analyzed, they are compatible with the concepts of genuine freedom and an open reality that this book articulates.

9

Personal Religion and the Openness of God

It is always appropriate to ask, "So what?" at the end of a theological discussion. All theology should be measured by its significance for personal religious experience. Throughout this discussion we have been sensitive to the criteria of biblical fidelity and logical consistency. We have tried to show that the open view of God is faithful to the biblical portrait of the Divine Being. We have also seen that it makes sense on logical grounds as well.

At the same time, we began our discussion by noticing the close connection between theology and personal experience. We have also remarked from time to time about the implications of the open view of God for personal religious experience. It will be appropriate to conclude our reflection on the openness of God by reviewing briefly its personal religious value. We shall not attempt a full-fledged theology of the Christian life from the perspective introduced here. Instead, we shall simply sketch a few of the lines along which such a theology conceivably could be developed.

A major contribution of the open view of God to personal religion is its support of creaturely significance. It does this in a number of ways, including an emphasis on individual uniqueness. God created beings who were themselves capable of creation in their appropriate sphere. By so doing He placed the future of the world to a large extent in creaturely hands. He allowed and invited His creatures to share in the work He had begun. Accordingly, our decisions have a creative quality about them. They are unique, irreplaceable. No one else can make quite the contribution we can to the ongoing course of events. Such an emphasis on creaturely freedom creates a strong sense of responsibility. This in turn provides a way to account for the emergence of evil in the world without ultimately blaming God for it.

An awareness of freedom also provides a basis for hope and optimism. If I am genuinely free, then outside influences never completely determine my situation. What I am may be largely due to factors over which I have had no control, but I need not allow these factors to determine my entire future. I can change my situation. I can grow beyond my present circumstances. This understanding has potential significance for the Christian counselor. We certainly do not want to blame individuals for problems that an unfortunate childhood, for example, has caused. But we can extend to them the hope that their future is open. Their own decisions now can largely determine their future.

The open view of God also supports a sense of personal significance by emphasizing God's sensitivity to our experiences. God takes an interest in every aspect of our lives. Nothing is too small or insignificant for Him to notice. He concerns Himself with everything that interests, concerns, and worries us. Moreover, God's experience reflects the actual course of our lives. What matters to us here and now makes a difference to God at this very moment. God feels not only *what* we feel, but also *as* we feel. He is intimately involved in the day-to-day course of our lives. Consequently, our different experiences have different effects upon God. He is pained with our suffering. He is exhilarated by our accomplishments. And He is pleased when we return His affection for us.

All this reflects the basic fact that God takes us seriously. He values our potential, and our failures to reach it disappoint Him. Because He respects our integrity as individuals, God ultimately accepts our decisions to respond or not to respond to Him. This is true both of our daily experiences and of our ultimate destiny.

He will not force Himself upon us. He will not save us against our wills. The concept of hell as the permanent separation of evildoers has its basis in God's high regard for creaturely integrity. It represents the final manifestation of His willingness to permit His creatures to make decisions that He profoundly regrets.

The openness of God also affirms the importance of human beings to each other. Our individual integrity has implications for interpersonal relationships as well as for our relationship with God. For one thing, it reminds us that we are free to affect the lives of other people. Our treatment of them will genuinely affect the course of their lives. And since we are open to each other, we each have the capacity to affect other human beings for better or worse. In this way, the open view of God and reality provides a basis for ethical concern. The recognition that we are all involved in the lives of one another has always played an important role in Christian thinking. However, the open view of God gives it a solid conceptual basis. The view presented here counteracts the individualism that occasionally afflicts conservative Christianity—the belief that the benefits accruing to an individual are the ultimate measure of the value of his actions.

We can see why the open view of God is important if we think of some of the reasons often given for missionary activity. Theological determinism offers little support for Christian mission. The view that every human being fulfills precisely the role that God assigns him in life removes the impetus from mission work. For in that case it is God who determines whether a person is saved or lost. Personal decision has nothing to do with it. The situation improves but little if we think of missionaries themselves as primarily benefiting from their activity. For in that case they also have the most to lose from a lack of missionary zeal. But when we think of other human beings as genuinely open to our influence, missionary activity receives a solid conceptual and motivational basis.

If our contribution to the lives of other people is both genuine and unique, then mission activity can make a profound difference in the ultimate destiny of human beings. Missionary endeavor is not merely the fulfillment of a God-assigned role that has no real impact on the course of events. Neither is it something undertaken primarily for our own benefit.

By emphasizing personal integrity the open view of God affirms not only our capacity to affect others but also our capacity to be affected by them. No one is entirely the product of external factors. Likewise, no one is himself entirely responsible for what he is. We would not be what we are without the contributions that other people have made to our lives. This recognition calls for a sense of gratitude on our part. It provides a helpful corrective to the "I did it my way" syndrome that afflicts many successful people. The fact is that no one achieves anything of value on his own. We are all indebted to the contributions that other people have made to our lives. And we would not be what we are without the unique influences that have been exerted upon us.

If we have the capacity to be enriched by the actions and decisions of other people, we are also vulnerable to mistreatment at their hands. Here we have a tragic demonstration of the enormous capacity of human beings to affect each other's lives. The vast proportion of human suffering comes from the abuse of other people. And we often wonder why God does not prevent such suffering. The strong sense of personal integrity implied by the open view of God provides an answer. God could not perpetually intervene to prevent mistreatment without basically altering the structure of interpersonal reality. Indeed, to do so would eliminate the possibility of positive influence as well.

In other words, an open reality involves risk. If we are genuinely able to affect the lives of other people for good, we are also able to affect them for evil. We saw earlier that moral freedom involves the presence of genuine alternatives. The possibility of moral good requires the risk of evil. The issue here is precisely the same. The possibility of interpersonal good involves the risk of mistreatment. Interpersonal freedom means that we are open to the contributions of others. It also means that we are vulnerable to their slights. God could not remove the latter without destroying freedom itself. They are part of the same thing.

Perhaps the most important implication of the openness of

God for personal religious experience is that it provides a basis for confidence and hope in the face of negative experiences. In our discussion of providence we saw that the open view of God relieves Him of all responsibility for the negative experiences of life. It does, however, affirm His capacity to work for good in every situation, no matter how bleak its prospects. We need both concepts in order to respond constructively to the tragedies of life.

Several years ago a woman of my acquaintance telephoned to break the news that her daughter, son-in-law, and their two children had perished in a plane crash. A few days later she related a friend's attempt to comfort her. He suggested that God had foreseen her loved ones would lose their religious commitment in the future. So He permitted their lives to end while they were still faithful to Him. We may excuse the man from rigorous theological accountability, given the stress of the situation, but we cannot help wondering how much reassurance he thought such a view of God would provide.

The idea that God is responsible for the suffering we experience, even if He brings difficulties upon us for our benefit, does not present us with an attractive picture of God. The notion that God plans for us to suffer, for whatever reason, provides little motivation to love Him. And it breaks down completely in the face of enormous amounts of suffering. It is difficult, for example, to see how any conceivable benefits could justify the suffering caused by extermination camps.

Our open view of God and reality presents the concept that God is not responsible for suffering. Suffering owes its existence to factors that oppose His will. But its occurrence does not leave Him helpless. He can act for good in the face of it. And He can accomplish certain things that would not have otherwise been possible. This understanding allows us to assign a certain meaning to tragic experiences. Yet we do not need to justify their occurrence or to maintain that it was all for the best that they happened.

Whether we are confronted with tragedy ourselves or attempt to encourage those who are, the open view of God enables us to do three things, and none of them involves the attempt to explain the purpose for suffering.

First, the open view of God affirms our sense of outrage at what has happened. Some things are simply wrong. They are not what God plans for us. Neither are they in our best interest. At times, people simply fall victim to unfortunate circumstances.

Second, the open view of God affirms that our experiences matter to God here and now. He is infinitely sensitive to what happens to us. It really makes a difference to Him. He appreciates to the fullest our loss, our grief, and our pain at the very time we suffer it. Indeed, His own sense of pain and loss far surpasses ours. There is nothing of value to us that does not mean a great deal to Him.

In other words, the open view of God provides a profound sense of divine sympathy. And a sense of sympathy often means more to people facing a loss than any attempt to fit it into some overall plan. The young son of a teacher died unexpectedly after a baseball injury. The professor later described a colleague's visit as the greatest help he received after the tragedy. His friend came to his office, sat down, and wept. After a while, his colleague excused himself and left. The display of shared grief meant far more than anything he might have said.

Third, the open view of God affirms that nothing lies beyond God's capacity to work for good. In response to any situation, however disastrous, God can work to our benefit. And these may be benefits that would not otherwise have existed. Such a recognition meets our natural desire to know that tragedies have not occurred in vain, that they count for something. And it does this without evoking the objectionable notions that God plans the tragedies to happen or that the benefits He derives from them always outweigh the loss they involve. American philosopher Josiah Royce says the essential idea of atonement is that of a new deed which transforms the meaning of a loss. But the new deed works not by undoing the loss but by bringing about a particular gain that could never have been achieved without it.[1] The open view of God supports this response to tragedies by denying God's

---

[1]Josiah Royce, *The Problem of Christianity* (Chicago: Henry Regnery Company, 1968), 1:309.

responsibility for everything that happens and by affirming His capacity to work for good in response to and in spite of them.

It's wrong. It matters. It counts for something. In confronting tragedy, we need the assurance that all three are true. The open view of God provides a basis for affirming each of them.

When it comes to the tragedies of our own creation, we especially need the reassurance that God can work for good in our behalf. And the open view of God provides a way of dealing with personal guilt. First of all, it affirms the reality of guilt by supporting a sense of personal responsibility. But secondly, it assures us that God can work for good even when we have deliberately and actively opposed His will. His creative power can transform the ultimate significance even of our sins. As a result, no portion of the life that is committed to God is entirely lost or worthless. A friend of mine came to college with an unsavory past behind him. But in the context of his Christian experience, the darkest part of his life acquired a positive meaning. Without glorifying himself or what he had done, he could describe his rescue from drug addiction in a way that generated hope for others facing the same problem.

God's infinite capacity to work for good provides a basis for confidence that His ultimate objectives for the world and for those who trust Him will finally be realized. If God can work for good in every situation, then He can use every development to promote His purposes. We can be assured that God now works to bring history to the goal He has in mind for it. Nothing can thwart the eventual realization of God's objectives, although many things can impede the progress toward these aims.

God's infinite resourcefulness guarantees the end of history. But since creaturely decisions also determine the actual course of history, other factors affect the time of its arrival. Several biblical passages, for example, relate the time of Christ's return to the church's fulfillment of the Gospel Commission (for example, Matt. 24:14). And at least one text suggests believers can hasten the coming of the day of God (2 Pet. 3:12). Consequently, the open view of reality supports a confidence that God's purposes will ultimately prevail. It also encourages a sense of responsibility for our part in the realization of His objectives. And this calls for a sense of urgency in fulfilling our part of the work.

The openness of God also affirms the importance of the daily Christian life. The notion of God's momentary sensitivity to our experiences reminds us that we should be momentarily receptive to His influence too. We are by nature developmental. What we are is not forever fixed by the past. We must, therefore, be constantly sensitive to the possibilities of the present situation and prepared to meet its challenges.

Moreover, the fulfillment of God's purposes for us on an individual basis requires our cooperation. This does not contradict the idea that our salvation is entirely a matter of divine grace. Salvation is a gift of which we are totally undeserving. But it does emphasize the fact that God never forces Himself upon us. He never overrides our freedom to accomplish His purposes, because He respects our integrity. So, while our participation in the work of salvation does not represent a contribution or a good work of which we can boast, God's saving activity in our lives requires our assent.

The openness of God gives integrity to the devotional life as well. With it, the question of whether prayer has any effect on God is not a source of perplexity, as it is on the traditional view. For if God is moment by moment sensitive to our experiences, then He is obviously affected by our prayers. Prayer contributes something to His experience that would not otherwise be there. We are not left with the unsatisfactory notion that prayer has no effect on God but is worth doing because it benefits us. Here again, we can avoid the trap of religious egocentricity.

At the same time, however, the openness of God does not provide an easy solution to the problem of intercessory prayer. We cannot imagine God's needing the excuse of a creaturely petition to act for good in the world. So it may be that such prayer sets in operation an imperceptible network of influence by which the other individual is genuinely affected by our concern for him. But we can only speculate as to how this is achieved. Perhaps intercessory prayer is a region of the Christian life in which it is better to trust our impulses than to seek an explanation.

The openness of God also provides a basis for appreciating corporate worship. God is receptive to our acts of worship. He is genuinely affected by them. Another consideration derives from the fact that we are radically open to the influence of other human beings. The devotional interaction of church members can generate an atmosphere that nothing on the individual level can duplicate. Corporate worship represents an irreplaceable part of the Christian life. The experience of meeting with others for prayers, hymns, exhortation, and celebration awakens levels of experience without which the religious life remains incomplete.

These remarks only hint at the many ways in which the open view of God can affect our religious experience. But they indicate that this concept can pass an important test of theological validity, namely, whether it makes any difference on the concrete personal level.

It seems, then, that the open view of God meets all the criteria of theological adequacy. It is biblically faithful. It is logically coherent. It is experientially significant. It not only solves many of the problems with the conventional conception of God's relation to the world, but it is richly suggestive as well. In relation to providence and prophecy it renders God's mysterious dealings with the world more wonderful than they first appeared. And it provides a basis for personal hope amid the darkest experiences of life.

In conclusion, the cluster of ideas discussed here provides a conceptual framework in which many of the basic affirmations of Christian faith can find a happy home. God's experience of the world is best conceived in terms of the openness of God.